The Power of Listening

How to Improve Relationships by Becoming an Active Listener

By

Damian Blair

Disclaimer

No part of this publication may be reproduced, stored in a retrieval system or transmitted in any form or by any means, electronic, mechanical, photocopying, recording, scanning or otherwise except as permitted under Sections 107 or 108 of the 1976 United States Copyright Act, without the prior written permission of the publisher.

While every precaution has been taken in the preparation of this book, the publisher assumes no responsibility for errors or omissions, or for damages resulting from the use of the information contained herein.

This book is for entertainment and informational purposes only. The views expressed are those of the author alone and should not be taken as expert instruction or commands. The reader is responsible for his or her own actions. Neither the author nor the publisher assumes any responsibility or liability whatsoever on behalf of the purchaser or reader of these materials. The reader is responsible for their own use of any products or methods mentioned in this publication.

This book includes information about products and equipment offered by third parties. As such, the author does not assume responsibility or liability for any third party products or opinions. Third party product manufacturers have not sanctioned this book, nor does the author receive any compensation from said manufacturers for sharing information regarding their products.

Table of Contents

Introduction

Have you ever found yourself in the middle of an argument with someone who just isn't getting it? No matter how hard you try to make your point, the other person doesn't seem to understand how you feel. They continue to misunderstand your point of view and you become even more frustrated, maybe even angry. Sometimes you feel as if they aren't even hearing the same language you are speaking. But since there isn't a language barrier, what's really going on?

Or, perhaps, you are the one on the other side of this conflict who is having trouble understanding the problem. You're listening to what the other person is saying but you don't see what the big deal is. You find no matter what you say to make things better, it only makes the situation worse. Your confusion grows, your response turns defensive and the sparks fly as the battle roars out of control.

Has it always been this way in our interpersonal relationships? Life is always evolving but it's usually for the better. Something has caused a shift in our ability to effectively communicate with family, friends, and co-workers. A change that has negatively impacted our interactions with the people around us. Finding the solution to a new problem often requires taking a look at how things used to be.

Advancement in communication technology has been both a blessing and a curse. It has allowed us to stay connected while miles apart. We are able to share the joys and heartaches of our daily lives with just one click. We can see each other live while living in different time zones. Without question, we are fully connected to the world via our online reality. Unfortunately, however, it has weakened our ability to effectively communicate face-to-face. We have gradually become emotionally disconnected from our family and friends in real life.

What happened to cause these relationship derailments when such advanced communication devices are right at our fingertips? This interpersonal disengagement is the result of spending more time with technology than interacting in person. It happens when parents text their kids who are in the same house rather than talk directly with them. Work exhausted you this week and you're just too tired to go upstairs. So what's the harm?

When parents rely too much on technology to communicate with their children they can miss signs of distress normally noticed in face-to-face interactions. For example, a text message to your child asking how their day went is likely to be met with a one-word response, more often in emoji form. You think "Great, everything's fine" and carry on with your evening.

Maybe school was fine but you can pick up on so many hidden signs of things not being fine if you know how to listen. A parent will only know who their child is by paying attention to everything they say and don't say. By communicating face-to-face, their tone of voice and body language will give context clues to their mood. You can then compare the words you hear in their answer to the signs they are giving off subconsciously. And if you have harnessed the power of listening, you will know whether or not their day went well.

Another example of situations in which technology has become a detriment to interpersonal communication occurs at family gatherings and social events. You've likely been at one of these where every attendee is on their device instead of visiting with the people sitting in the same room. Each person is absorbed in their own world of social media almost unaware of the world around them.

It's almost as if our phone has become an extension of our hand as we show pictures and video clips to one another. It's as if we have developed a new language of personal connection consisting of sharing and resharing the same memes. We've gone from the days of getting to know one another through talking to comparing lives through social media status. Do we really learn anything about one another through this exchange? A little perhaps, but not nearly as much as when we talk to be heard and listen to understand.

Even if you haven't experienced either of the previous situations, surely you've watched sports or events on television where a majority of the patrons are looking into their phones. We have become so attached to our virtual lives that we're missing what's happening right in front of us. Watch closely the next time you see a group of kids getting off the school bus. What are they doing? Without fail, the vast majority of them are looking into a phone or tablet device as they are walking home.

Strangely enough, the more advanced our communication technology has become, the less effective our communication has gotten. Beyond the reasons just illustrated, the way in which we communicate has reverted back to simpler times when we spoke in grunts and painted pictographs on caves. Texting shorthand and the use of emojis in place of emotions have inadvertently minimized their revelatory meaning.

Text messages, social media posts, and emails only convey the words of the statement. They generally lack the tone of voice we hear when someone speaks in fear or in anger. We miss out on the visual emotive cues we see during direct interpersonal communication. Words on a screen cannot express the hurt you see in someone's eyes who has been betrayed. Without these important context clues, we struggle to grasp the intent of the messenger and often the real meaning of the message.

Our dependence on instant communication has resulted in forgetting how to talk to each other in person. Technology has given us the power to be ever more selfish in our communication with others, believing what we have to say is more important. Modern communication has made it easier to "talk" over someone by blasting them with messages. It has even become more convenient to ignore the other person outright by not responding, which has created a whole new level of the silent treatment.

It goes without saying that not all conflicts can be avoided. However, being prepared and having a clear head can keep conversations moving in a positive direction towards a resolution. Used correctly, the tools in this book will increase the strength of your personal and professional relationships. You will learn the quantitative difference between hearing the words of what someone said and listening to the meaning of what they are saying. This book will help you to harness the power of active listening.

Your learning quest begins with a closer look at the roles of speaker and listener during a combative interpersonal conversation. By knowing what is expected of each player, a common goal can often be reached amicably. Being without knowledge of the other person's feelings or intent will put communication in peril, frequently resulting in unresolved conflict or damage to the relationship.

By the end of this first step, you will possess an awareness of the distractions that impede your interpersonal communications. You will be more conscious of the unconscious message your body language is speaking to others. The information I provide in the first chapter will show you how to get prepared before beginning to listen. Once you have gained these insights, the exploration continues with an introduction to the three levels of listening.

In the next leg of the journey, I will illustrate the significant characteristics of the different levels of listening. Beginning with the most common level, listening in spurts, I will demonstrate how the message is misconstrued when you only hear bits and pieces. This portion of the trip may seem intimidating with all the ground we'll cover, but don't get discouraged. The concepts may sound foreign at first glance but by the end of this stage, the examples will feel all too familiar.

The primary focus of Chapter Two is the effectiveness of the tool, active listening. This chapter will provide a detailed breakdown of the technical components involved in this second level of listening. You will learn about both the verbal and nonverbal elements that influence our communication with others. You will become more familiar with the communication enhancers associated with active listening. In addition, I will cover the various stumbling blocks that impede one's ability to actively listen.

Most importantly, you will come away with a selection of active listening styles to improve your interpersonal communication skills with everyone in your life. I will provide relatable examples to demonstrate the four types of active listening and how each one can be used at work and at home. These scenarios will address how to use each style in your own life and give you specific answers on how to handle a situation.

Chapter Three takes us down the rugged path of emotion towards the third level of listening, empathic listening. The key to reaching this highest level of listening is knowing the difference between empathy and sympathy. Solving this riddle will take an open mind and willingness to see life from another point of view. Empathic listening isn't about pity for the other person but rather the ability to feel their suffering with an understanding of their point of view and a desire to help.

In order to fully understand the other person's message and intent, you must be able to relate to the emotions they are feeling. If you are unable to recognize how they are feeling, you won't have the complete picture of the message they are trying to convey. These missed cues of emotion are often at the heart of our combative interpersonal communication failures.

Once you are more in tune with the feelings of others through empathy, I will teach you how to speak with an empathic response and why it is important to the listening process. This level of communication goes beyond merely knowing how the person is feeling. It involves a complete empathic submersion into experiencing the conflict from your opponent's mindset. An empathic listener hears more than just the words being spoken. When you let go of your judgments and feel the other person's suffering as your own, you gain a new perspective on the conflict.

In this next portion of the book, I discuss the three types of empathic listening and illustrate situations best suited for each. I will cover the powerful effect that speaking with empathy can have on your personal and professional relationships. In turn, you will learn how to step out of the advice-giving role and step into the position of the collaborative problem solver.

The full power of active listening with empathy cannot be obtained without the final step of validation. We all have something we want to say and we want someone to hear our words and understand how we feel. As humans, we also have a strong desire for an affirmation from others that what we are feeling and experiencing is normal. Nothing is as lonely as the feeling we're the only one.

A big part of why people struggle with avoiding combative interpersonal communication is due to a lack of personal boundaries. Many of us have that desire to fix the problem for the other person rather than lead them to find their own solution. While often done with the best intent, telling someone how to fix their problem invalidates their feelings and changes the dynamic of the conversation.

Personal boundaries are those invisible lines in relationships that define our expectations of behavior from others. They are the levels of tolerance each of us has with regard to aspects of communication in the relationship. Healthy active listening requires an understanding of one's personal boundaries and the boundaries of other people.

Too often when we argue, we cross those personal boundaries and our words become weapons of anger. When we know the person well, we attack them where they are weak instead of trying to build them back up. On the opposite end of the spectrum, we find ourselves waving the white flag of defeat and accepting the person's harmful situation as the new norm.

Relationships, whether personal or professional, should feel balanced and equal. Living in a constant power struggle to be heard is a toxic environment for the mind and spirit. Being in a situation where your thoughts and actions are constantly judged or ignored is unhealthy and drives down self-esteem. The information covered here will give you the guidance to ensure your personal boundaries are established. I will provide suggestions on ways to communicate to others what those boundaries are and help you to stand firm in your convictions.

I will show you how a single sentence response can express support, encouragement, and interest in what the other person is saying. Through examples, I will demonstrate how validating statements reduce the level of emotional pain and suffering the speaker is experiencing. In this chapter, we will compare the outcomes of using good validation statements versus bad validation.

In the final chapter of the book, I will consolidate everything we have covered into a five-step technique to reach the highest level of active empathic listening. You will have a step-by-step guide through a multitude of real-life scenarios to help illustrate the plan in action. I will highlight the key components of effective listening in each situational example to solidify the lesson being taught.

As a couples therapist, I witnessed people experience radical breakthroughs once they understood what was holding them back. I saw as they recognized how the changes in their communication style positively impacted their relationships at home. In time, I noticed how active listening created a beneficial side effect of improving personal relationships outside of the marital relationship.

So encouraged by this life-enhancing method of communication, I expanded my practice of psychotherapy. I began to help clients address the interpersonal conflicts they were experiencing with other family members and eventually, work relationships.

This book was written to give clear direction and guidance for improving how to listen to the people in our lives. The lessons within will lead you to build better relationships at home, at work, and everywhere in between. The Power of Listening is designed to lead you down a path of self-awareness and self-improvement. It is also made to serve as a reminder of the role we play in the conflicts we encounter.

This book will give you the power to be mindful of your own words and actions through understanding the process of healthy communication. As they say, the first step to improving yourself is recognizing there is a problem. By choosing this book, you have made a conscious decision to make a personal change towards growth and self-improvement. When we care enough about the quality of our relationships, we put in the extra effort to make a change for the better. Active empathic listening requires a selflessness that has faded into the background.

If you're not ready to take action and be accountable for your own communication flaws, then this book isn't for you. You will not find any quick fix patch jobs in this manuscript. Replacing years of bad communication habits is a work in progress that begins with identifying the root of the conflict. It requires relearning how to listen with openness and empathy.

This book will not teach you how to manipulate other people into doing what you want. It is not a book of tricks to make people listen but a guidebook to becoming a better listener. What you will learn can be put towards improving every relationship in your life. But it will take self-discipline and accountability to make a difference.

Changing how you communicate is almost like learning to speak a new language. Before you can become fluent, you need to become familiar with the vocabulary used. Likewise, this book will define unfamiliar terms in a way that makes their meaning clear. I will take each lesson and build upon it the same way you build words into sentences when learning to speak.

When you're finished reading this book, you will have a better view of the inner workings of communication. I will give you all of the means to create monumental breakthroughs in your personal and professional life. All I ask from you is to make a commitment to work hard, stay the course, and strive to be the powerful listener we all are capable of being.

Chapter One: Preparing to Listen

We communicate with others to either share factual information or to express how we are feeling about a situation. Most of our conversations consist of the first type, like telling your spouse dinner is ready or announcing that you are leaving for work. Very little pre-thought or planning is needed for these types of interactions. Nor is there a need for the expression of feelings when communication is the straightforward sharing of a fact.

But the types of talks where you want to address an issue with another person are a different kind of conversation. One where you spend time thinking about what you want to say and how to say it. As humans, we want to be heard. So why is it that we don't put as much effort into preparing to listen when someone has something important to say to us?

Preparing to listen effectively begins with understanding the difference between hearing and listening. It takes knowing what it means to be active and empathic. With this information, you will begin to see the power of listening. You will discover that the better prepared you are to listen, the more successful that interaction and, ultimately, the relationship will be.

In this chapter, I will teach you the invaluable difference between hearing and listening. You will be able to understand how each plays a role in our interpersonal communication. I will pinpoint the listening distractors that negatively impact the way we communicate. With this knowledge, you will learn how to identify the obstacles that are preventing you from listening.

I will demonstrate the importance of both correctly identifying the message and being able to relate to it. You will discover exactly what information your body language contributes to the conversation. Through examples, you will see how our nonverbal signals can influence the message being sent. I will also show you examples of good and bad listening to help illustrate the tools you need to become a more powerful listener.

Hearing Words and Listening to Meaning

Most people tend to use the words hearing and listening interchangeably. And while they do have a very similar definition in most contexts, combative interpersonal communication reveals differing interpretations. When used in the context of conflict resolution, hearing and listening are vastly different.

Hearing the words someone is speaking is akin to hearing a noise. Our ears take in the sounds of the letters being spoken. Those sounds are transmitted to our brains to be interpreted as words that we recognize. In this sense, hearing is more in tune with the physiology of the ear performing its job. Listening, on the other hand, goes a step further.

When we listen to the words being spoken, we make an effort of understanding the meaning of the message. Listening involves making the connection between the speaker's words and the intent of the person speaking. It requires making a conscious effort to give the speaker your full attention in order to perceive the situation accurately.

Let's take a look at an example to help illustrate the critical difference between hearing words and listening to the message. You're at home checking work emails when your daughter pops into the kitchen for a snack. She begins to tell you about how a classmate spread false rumors about her online. You reply with generic responses and she continues to vent her frustrations. After she seems to be done talking, you give some basic parental advice about ignoring it and she goes off to her room.

You may have been hearing what your daughter had to say but were you truly listening if your mind was focused on work? When you are unable to give your full attention to someone, you are telling that person what they have to say isn't important to you. And if you don't value what the person says, you essentially are saying you don't value that person.

Had you taken a moment to put aside work to effectively listen to your daughter, you would have realized she was in need of more personal advice. You would have seen the frustration in her eyes when she described the lies being spread about her and how she felt humiliated at school. We may think we only listen with our ears, but we hear so much more when we use our other senses.

This example shows how important it is to pay attention to more than just the words being spoken in order to understand the message. It also illustrates how listening to someone requires using more than just your ears. When you look at the person speaking, you will see their facial expressions that can help relay how they really feel about what they are saying to you.

While external distractions are often to blame for not listening effectively, arguments reveal another way hearing and listening are different. For this scenario, your spouse wants to take the family on a camping trip for this year's vacation. You, on the other hand, despise camping after that horrible trip back in college and swore to do it never again.

Your spouse tries to tell you all of the great things about the trip and how fun it would be for the kids. Meanwhile, all you are thinking about is the bad experience you had and anything positive your spouse says about the idea, you immediately have a negative story to counter it with.

In this situation, you're hearing your spouse's words related to camping but you're not listening to how positive an impact camping had on them growing up. You became so focused on the one bad experience you had that you couldn't see positive memories your spouse wants to create with your own family. You only heard what you chose to hear.

What this distinction between hearing and listening shows you is how much having common ground can affect your willingness to listen. This example illustrates that how well you listen to the message depends on whether you perceive the message as something you want to hear or would rather tune-out. In terms of our interpersonal conflicts, this occurs when we are unable to relate to the emotion the other person is experiencing.

It happens when one or both of you are not willing to listen to something you're not used to hearing. You don't relate to the message being broadcast so you are unable to feel the emotion attached to the message. In extreme cases of disconnect, you risk damaging a relationship when failing to see the problem from the other's point of view.

Interpersonal communication will only reach its maximum potential when both individuals master the two factors of listening. Correctly identifying the message being sent to your ears is vital to resolving the conflict. It's almost impossible to make repairs to something when you haven't correctly diagnosed the situation. Adding fuel to your car isn't going to help it go if the problem is a flat tire.

Another key to conflict resolution is being able to relate to the problem through a shared emotional bond. This makes it much easier to listen when it's something you understand on a personal level. Resolving a conflict that is mutually understood will almost certainly be mutually beneficial if success is reached.

Once you understand the difference between hearing what someone is saying and listening to what they are trying to convey, you will be ready to take the next step of preparing to listen. Identifying what is impeding your ability to listen requires examining your environment and your mind. I will address the behaviors and beliefs that create these blocks. As you master each lesson, you will be able to make the necessary changes in both your thoughts and actions as they relate to healthy interpersonal communication.

Roadblocks to Listening

Before you can begin to listen, you must first address those things that prevent you from being able to do so effectively. These impediments to communication can be put into one of two categories: internal distractions and external distractions. These two types of interference occur in different ways but have the same result in communication breakdown.

Internal distractions refer to the thoughts occurring in your mind during the encounter that prevent you from paying attention to what is being said. We have become so self-focused in our fast-paced lives that we find ourselves rushing to respond before hearing the question. It happens more often than we realize.

You're at the office on Friday and the boss stops by your desk to tell you about the important meeting on Monday. Try as you might, you find yourself thinking about the big game this weekend instead of listening. Your boss asks your opinion on what defense strategy you would use in the upcoming case and you reply with a statement about linebackers and defensive ends. It's obvious you were not listening.

When it comes to internal distractions, the most problematic one is the belief that what you have to say is more important. Instead of listening to what the other person is saying, the self-focused individual is thinking about what they want to say next. They have already decided the outcome of the conflict, so, instead of remaining open-minded, they continue their rehearsed argument.

Unfortunately, when you become so focused on making your case known, you miss out on the opportunity to see another point of view. You prevent yourself from gaining new insight into the conflict or being able to understand the other side of the disagreement. Even worse than that, your refusal to pay attention will prevent you from recognizing you're actually in agreement.

External distractions are things that disrupt your ability to listen. Items such as your cell phone, television, and other electronics take your attention away from the conversation. It also tells the other person that they are not as important as whatever has your focus. Even something as innocuous as checking the time on your watch can be perceived as a lack of interest in the now.

Creating an environment free from external distractions can be accomplished by simply turning your phone to silent or closing your laptop. Shutting off the television or radio will clear the air of noise interference. If the conversation is happening at work, close the office door to block out the ambient noise of co-workers. It will also convey the confidentiality of the conversation, which will instill confidence in being able to speak openly.

The external element that has the biggest impact on our interpersonal communication is body language. It has the unique ability to be either an impediment to the conversation or a positive influence on conflict resolution. When interpreted correctly, body language can reveal how a person truly feels emotionally.

Body Language Messages

Research has found that body language is the biggest factor of message conveyance. According to Mehrabian's Communication Model, body language is responsible for over 90% of interpersonal communication. The remaining percentage is divided up between the words you choose and the tone of voice in which they are spoken.

Body language gives the listener a visual indicator for gauging the sentiment of the message. Our posture, facial expressions, and hand gestures reveal clues to our current thoughts and emotions. How we position our body while sitting or standing can indicate whether we are tense or relaxed. Where our gaze is focused can disclose our lack of interest or show we're intrigued.

These postures, positions, and expressions of the face are near impossible to convey when communicating via text and email. Digital communication limits us to animated GIFs and an array of emojis to express how we feel. In addition, these electronic impersonations of emotion are far more easily misinterpreted than direct interactions. But even in person, we can misread the context clues before us.

Reaching your full listening potential will require you to familiarize yourself with the message being spoken through body language. This nonverbal form of communication will help you determine the initial mood of the other person. Are they expressing an open posture that welcomes conversation? Or does their body language indicate an unwillingness to communicate?

Closed body language indicates signs of displeasure, lack of interest, or lack of engagement in the conversation. What you will see when someone feels this way includes arms folded across the chest like a shield blocking their heart. Their facial expressions will appear tense or they may show little discernible emotion.

People expressing resistance to the conversation will turn their bodies away in an effort to avoid direct confrontation. Often they will take on a submissive posture with their head down to minimize eye contact. This type of body language is the expression of their feelings of stress, anger, or nervousness. It can also be an indication of indifference, or an 'I don't care' kind of attitude.

This closed body language is often seen during uncomfortable conversations such as giving someone constructive criticism in a performance review. Another prime example where you will see signals of displeasure occurs when attending to an unhappy customer. Mediating a contract negotiation can also create the level of tension closed body language brings out of some people.

In more personal situations, you may be met with crossed arms and disinterest from someone who isn't ready to be confronted. Whether it's as severe as an addiction or as minor as getting your kid to clean their room, a disengaged listener will show the same nonverbal clues. Once you're able to recognize these signs, you'll be more prepared to interpret the full message they are trying to convey to you.

Open body language sends a positive message of being relaxed, comfortable, and in control of your feelings. A posture of sitting or standing up tall with hands at your sides shows that you are confident and non-combative. Relaxed shoulders while head held high show signs of comfort that will pair well with calm and pleasant facial expressions.

Hands are one of the most communicative body parts and where you place them, hold different meanings. Putting your hands on your hips when in a standing position shows an aggressive stance and can be perceived as intimidation. Inserting them into your pockets, on the other hand, puts off a vibe of disinterest. Other things to avoid with regard to your hands include fidgeting with your face or hair as this conveys deception and not being trustworthy.

Eye contact is another way to express open body language and a willingness to communicate. You show the listener you are interested in what they are saying when you look them in the eye. The problem people experience with regard to maintaining eye contact is not overdoing it. Learning how to briefly break eye contact so as not to be staring the other person down takes practice.

A nod of the head is another positive open body language tool to communicate interest and understanding. It tells the other person that you are acknowledging what they are saying. It also encourages that person to continue speaking which keeps the conversation going. Likewise, the slow shaking of one's head can indicate feelings of empathy and compassion.

Body language can be used to guide the other person from closed to open through a method called mirroring. This nonverbal communication tool is helpful for diffusing high-intensity emotional conflicts. By mimicking the other person's body language, you can visually reflect how they are feeling to help ease their anxiety. Subtlety is essential when using mirroring so as not to make them uncomfortable by copying their every move. When done correctly, it will strengthen the interpersonal bond of your communication.

The 3 Levels of Listening

The final step towards preparing to listen is an understanding of the three levels of listening. At the base of this listening-pyramid is basic listening. Sometimes referred to as listening in spurts, level one listening is the most common in our daily lives. In level one, we pay attention just enough to hear the sounds.

Active listening is the next level and requires more effort from the listener. Listening actively involves staying focused on the speaker. It requires the listener to pay attention to the details being spoken and to watch for the unspoken clues of context. Being an active listener means showing the speaker what they have to say is important.

Empathic listening goes one step further and is the highest level of effective listening. Listening empathically means you understand the speaker from their perspective. An empathic listener is able to feel the emotions being experienced by the speaker. When you listen with empathy, you put yourself in the other person's shoes instead of trying to change their view to yours.

Level One Listening

You use level one listening when you listen to the radio while driving to work or school. You pay attention to everything around you in order to be able to hear that emergency vehicle coming up behind you. Level one listening includes those times when you kick back and listen to the pitter-patter of rain or the crashing of the waves.

While level one listening does serve a purpose, it is the least effective level for interpersonal communication. One of two types of listening occurs when you try to use level one listening for conversations and conflict resolution. The first type is called listening without comprehension and the other is listening with unconfirmed comprehension.

One example of listening without comprehension is that all too familiar situation where someone has been speaking to you but you were not fully paying attention. You hear them talking as you're watching television. Then you realize the person that was speaking is waiting for you to respond. Based on your lack of reaction they ask if you heard what they said.

Perplexed, your mind scrambles to piece together the few words you think you heard to formulate a logical answer. You try to remember what day it is to see if there may be a clue to this request. You stall by mumbling some incoherent babble about taking out the trash. Too late, you're busted. 'You never listen!' they yell as they leave in a huff.

Other reasons listening without comprehension can occur is when the listener is not interested in the topic or is focused on an unrelated topic. In addition, our ability to comprehend what we are hearing decreases when emotional intensity increases. If a listener feels threatened or under attack, they are less likely to want to listen, and in turn, will be unable to fully comprehend the conversation.

A mismatch of words to body language will undoubtedly create confusion for the listener trying to understand the message. People have a tendency to trust body language over words. And for some people, a misunderstanding of the message simply occurs because of auditory factors. These elements include hearing or speech impairments and heavy or unfamiliar accents.

Listening with unconfirmed comprehension is a different kind of listening impediment. This type of level one listening is a side effect of our brain's ability to think at a much faster rate of speed than we can speak. What that means is when someone is speaking the brain of the listener is racing ahead in an attempt to predict what the speaker is trying to convey.

This thinking ahead can become troublesome in a number of ways, however, when the listener's brain makes an incorrect assumption. What often happens is the listener is so confident they know what the speaker is trying to say that they interject their own thought into the conversation. Unfortunately for them, they missed an important detail by not giving full attention to the speaker's message. If the listener had been listening instead of trying to out-think the speaker, they would have heard all of the pertinent information. When we try to foretell what the speaker is trying to say, we can come to the wrong conclusion about the message. Not to mention it is extremely rude to interrupt someone when they are speaking.

These misunderstandings from making assumptions also occur when two people understand a different meaning for the same thing. This can happen when the common meaning of a word has changed over time. This type of misunderstanding can also be the result of the listener and speaker having a different perception of the words or phrasing being used in the message.

Level Two - Active Listening

In order to reach a mutual point of understanding, you must move up from the ineffective first level of listening. Active listening is the next level in the listening pyramid. At this level, the listener consciously engages in actions that increase their ability to understand the meaning of the speaker's message.

As the sides of a pyramid rise, they come closer together until meeting at the same point. Likewise, as you ascend the levels of listening, you will find it is much easier to converge on a solution. When individuals are working together at the same listening level, problem-solving comes together so much faster.

In the next chapter, I will explain in greater detail the importance of playing an active role during interpersonal communication. I will share examples to illustrate the technical components of active listening. You will learn how effective nonverbal actions, like smiling, can positively influence the conversation. You'll also see how slight adjustments in how you listen can greatly impact both interpersonal communication and the relationship as a whole. I will also teach you several verbal tools you can use that confirm to the speaker they are being heard and understood.

Level Three - Empathic Listening

In chapter three, we will explore the highest level-- listening with empathy. You will gain insight into what it means to be an empathic listener and why it is so critical to interpersonal communication. I will show you the significance of knowing the difference between the pity of sympathy and the sincerity of empathy.

Empathic listening will give you the power to see the situation from the speaker's point of view. It will provide you with the tools to discern the entire message being conveyed by the speaker. By the end of chapter three, you will be able to recognize where your level of listening falls. You will also know how to tell at what level others are listening to you.

Chapter One Recap

❖ Hearing differs from listening in that our ears take in the sounds and words we hear while listening involves using our mind to infer their meaning.

❖ Listening effectively takes both a quiet environment and a quieted mind. We must eliminate the roadblocks of listening by identifying the external and internal noise that distracts us from hearing and listening.

❖ Body language is the unspoken expression of our true feelings. Learning how to read the signals being received and understanding the signals we send can enhance our level of communication.

❖ Day-to-day interactions mostly involve listening at the first and most basic level. Rising up to the more effective levels of active and empathic listening is essential to making deeper personal connections with others.

The power of listening comes from being willing to put forth the effort required. It comes from learning to be less focused on the self while acquiring the complete knowledge of productive communication. As children we learn how to speak to express ourselves. From that moment on, we continue to discover the intricacies of every aspect of interpersonal communication with active and empathic conversation.

Chapter 2: How to Be an Active Listener

We all have moments in our lives when we just need someone to listen. You had a bad day and want to vent about your jerk of a boss. Or maybe you have a great idea for a story you're writing and want to test it out on an audience of one. Whatever your reason, you have a certain expectation of the listener. You want someone to pay attention. You want them to really get what you're trying to tell them. You want to feel like someone else understands your anguish of mistreatment at work or the joy of a breakthrough in your writer's block. What you want is an active listener.

This chapter will first define what it means to be an active listener and what this level of listening accomplishes. We will look at the physicality of active listening by examining both the verbal and non-verbal components. I will provide you with the tools you need to become an effective active listener. Most importantly, this chapter identifies the communication obstacles and enhancers that impact our ability to actively listen.

What is Active Listening?

Active listening is a set of skills that take time and effort to learn. It's an art that takes practice in order to masterfully wield the tools of effective communication. It requires the listener to remove their own beliefs, biases, and feelings from the conversation equation. An active listener must be able to clear their mind of any preconceived opinions about the speaker or the message in order to observe from the speaker's mindset.

We all experience life in our own way giving us each a unique perspective. Your life had influences that helped define your view of the world. Likewise, everyone you encounter has had events in their lives that formed their perception of how the world works. We may all live on the same planet, but what we live through defines how we see life.

.

Being an active listener means you are able to step outside of your worldview and see things from the other person's perspective. Your mind must remain focused on the messenger with your feet firmly planted in their world. Actively listening means paying attention to the words of the speaker and their understood meaning. It also means being alert to the tone of voice being used in the conversation.

As an active listener, you know to watch for the non-verbal clues a speaker unconsciously reveals during the conversation. These hints can help you to decipher how the speaker is feeling when the message is unclear or unfamiliar. Paying attention to the speaker's body language, facial expressions, and hand gestures can give you, the active listener, a clearer representation of the message.

Once the speaker has finished talking, you can confirm that you are understanding the meaning of the speaker's message. You can reiterate the essential elements of the speaker's communication to be sure the message was received correctly. In other words, as an active listener, it is up to you to make certain you have accurately put together all of the pieces of the communication puzzle.

To be an active listener means you are able to connect with others where they are, as opposed to making them see things your way. It's an advanced communication technique that creates a safe and honest environment for facilitating relationships. Active listening doesn't require us to agree with one another but it does provide an opportunity to examine the unfamiliar.

When you become an active listener, you provide an open forum where the speaker feels free to express themselves honestly. Your focus on their experience without personal bias increases their comfort level and leads to a willingness to share more with you. Through this deeper connection, you, the active listener, will have a greater understanding of the motivations, drive, and needs of the people in your life. From there, you will be able to establish profoundly more meaningful relationships.

The Physicality of Active Listening

How can you tell if someone is actively listening? What does an active listener look like? Perhaps, most importantly, when does an active listener speak and what do they say? These questions can all be answered by looking at the physicality of active listening. By taking note of what an active listener looks like, you will be able to see when someone is engaged being spoken to. Even more, you will learn what signals you are giving or failing to give the speaker when you are the listener.

In addition to what you do as an active listener to show you're paying attention, when and how you reply to the speaker is also important. This aspect of active listening physiology is equally as impactful as the nonverbal components. Learning how to become the most effective active listener will require you to completely understand both the verbal and nonverbal aspects of this technique.

Nonverbal Signs of Active Listening

Believe it or not, you have the power to foster or destroy a conversation without ever uttering a word. You are able to convey your interest in what the speaker is saying through action. Likewise, you can also exhibit hints of disinterest or boredom through your behavior. It may seem difficult to tell if someone is actively listening to you, but when someone isn't listening, we can usually tell almost immediately.

Eye Contact

Nonverbal signs that indicate you are actively listening begin with your eyes. As an active listener, you maintain focus on the speaker by looking at the person speaking. Eye contact tells the speaker you are paying attention to them visually. It tells them you are seeing their facial expressions and hand gestures that accentuate their verbal message.

When you make eye contact with the speaker, it is a brief meeting of the eyes that confirms you are engaged in the conversation. Your eye contact indicates to the speaker you are listening and acknowledging their speaking. Avoiding eye contact, on the other hand, gives the impression that you are being elusive or feel uncomfortable with the conversation. Some see this avoidance of looking them in the eye as a sign of rudeness, arrogance, or guilt.

Keeping your eyes on the speaker will also increase your ability to stay focused on the message by avoiding visual distractions. Diverting your eyes to check your phone or the clock takes your mind off the speaker and thus focused on yourself. Not only do you risk missing something key to the conversation, being distracted can make the speaker feel they are not as important to you as whatever it is that has your attention.

Making eye contact with the speaker helps your brain to process information about the person speaking to you. Important aspects such as their name or the company they work for will be easier to remember when you make eye contact as they speak. What they look like, how they sound, and the tone of their message are all easier to detect and remember when you use proper eye contact.

On the other side of seeing, eye contact from the speaker will influence your behavior. You become more self-aware when you know you're being watched. You are more conscientious of your actions and behaviors when the speaker meets your gaze. Our sense of being judged and evaluated by others from eye contact can affect what we say and how we react to the person speaking.

Smiling

Smiling is one of our most primal communication tools for expressing the emotion of contentment. You smile when being introduced to someone to show you're happy to meet them. You smile when you run into a friend you haven't seen in a while because you're so glad to see they're doing well. When you smile, you experience a positive chain reaction in your brain. It starts in your brainstem where your brain tells your muscles what to do. Once the muscles send back confirmation they smiled, the brainstem rewards you with feelings of euphoria. How cool is that? You have a positive experience that makes you smile because you feel good. Then you feel even better thanks to your brain's reward system, prompting you to smile even more.

When you take into consideration that smiling tends to be contagious, it has the power to help improve the mood of anyone you meet. Your role as an active listener is to help the speaker be more relaxed and at ease and what better way to improve the energy of the conversation than with a smile. Smiling not only releases feel-good hormones but also reduces the feelings of stress for both you and the speaker. But it has to be genuine because most people will pick up on a forced smile.

You can practice smiling in the mirror to get an idea of how your smile looks to others. One way to work on perfecting it is to think about your happiest moment. This method can be used to practice before an interview or when meeting someone for the first time. Your smile can say a lot about how you feel, as well as, how you feel about the other person.

Posturing

Body posturing refers to the way you are standing or sitting during a conversation. Your posture of standing or sitting tall with your shoulders back and head held high gives the impression of strength. It physically displays the muscular fortitude of standing strong, which reflects you having a strong character and being a real stand-up individual.

How you position your body in relation to the speaker can indicate how effective you are listening. As an active listener, lean towards the speaker to indicate you are engaged and interested in what they have to say. Someone who doesn't care about what's being said or is oppositional to the message will put space between themself and the speaker. Leaning away from the other person is a visual distancing cue to illustrate the differing of opinion.

The positioning of your feet can also give indications of your stance on the subject. Placing your feet together is symbolic of obedience as seen when the military stand at attention or when a child is being addressed by an upset parent. Having your feet spaced apart shows you are relaxed and open to communication Your feet will also give clues to where your mind is through the direction in which it points. When your mind is focused on the speaker, your foot may be pointing towards them. If, however, your mind is ready to leave, your foot may point towards the nearest exit.

Body posture can also give clues to your level of confidence, or lack of confidence. For example, sitting with your ankles crossed typically means you are unsure or insecure about the conversation. Open posturing sets the gauge for your level of confidence. The more confident you are, the more open your body posture tends to be.

Body Mirroring

Your purpose as an active listener is to make a personal and emotional connection with the speaker. In using the technique of body mirroring, you are actively modeling your body language and posturing after the other person. It is your non-verbal way of saying, 'I feel the same way as you about XYZ'. Body mirroring can be used to build rapport and trust with someone by mirroring their body language, tone of voice, and even their breathing pattern.

Body mirroring, also known as limbic synchrony is hard-wired in your brain as a means of connecting emotionally to others. Science has discovered neurons in your brain that react in the same way whether you are doing the activity or seeing it done by someone else. Not only do the neurons replicate the action being seen, but they are able to mirror the emotions associated with the action.

This can explain why, for some of us, seeing someone else cry when they are upset can make you cry and feel their emotional pain. Empathy occurs because your brain is able to interpret the speaker's emotion from their body language. By mirroring their body language and activating your natural limbic synchrony, you are able to feel what the speaker is feeling.

Lack of Distraction
In our fast-paced, got-to-reply-now lifestyles, we are constantly bombarded by distractions. Your phone beeps, dings, and sings for every alert, email, and phone call. It's no wonder you're not fully paying attention to the person right in front of you or on the other end of the phone.

How can you even hear the conversation with so many auditory interruptions? As an active listener, you are responsible for accurately deciphering the speaker's message. And the only way you can do so is by shutting out and shutting off all external noise that could distract you from what's most important-- listening.

Distractions are disruptive as well as disrespectful to the speaker. Your quick check of an email tells the speaker you don't feel what they are saying is important enough to warrant your full attention. You convey to the speaker that they are less worthy of your time than what has you distracted. And that disrespect will most certainly have a negative impact on the relationship you have with the other person.

Verbal Signs of Active Listening

As an active listener, you have six verbal response options to choose from that confirm to the speaker you are listening attentively. Each of these verbal options, when used correctly, will assure the speaker their message is coming across to you clearly. In addition, you are able to use these signs of active listening to better understand anything that you found unclear or unfamiliar.

Positive Reinforcement

The first verbal sign that you can use during active listening is called positive reinforcement. An active listener uses positive reinforcement to verbally express their affirmation of the speaker's message. Using words and phrases like 'nice', 'yes', or 'indeed' reinforces to the speaker that what they are saying is agreeable to you, the listener. It gives an indication that you understand and feel the same way.

These positive and brief statements can be inspiring, however, you should use them sparingly. Used too often, they can become distracting to the speaker, causing them to lose focus. In addition, overuse of positive reinforcement gives the impression you are being too agreeable and can be perceived as a disingenuous 'yes man or woman' who always agrees.

Remembering

Remembering and being able to retell key information from the speaker's message is another verbal sign of attentive active listening. Our minds are always taking in information from everywhere and trying to remember it all is impossible. When you are able to recall important details from the message, it shows the speaker you were paying attention and encourages them to continue talking.

When you make the effort to commit to memory identifiable aspects of both the speaker and their message, it shows a commitment to the individual. Something as simple as remembering the speaker's name shows them you see them as a person worthy of being heard. Keeping the information about the speaker and their message committed to memory will be even more invaluable to the development of the relationship in future encounters.

Questioning and Clarification

The next two verbal signs of attentive active listening you can use to gain understanding are questioning and clarifying. These two verbalizations both use question statements but for different goals. When you use questioning, the speaker is prompted to elaborate in an effort to elicit more details. You can also use clarifying to ensure you have correctly understood the meaning of the message.

An example of a questioning statement would be, 'Can you tell me more about how your budget will be implemented?' This tells the speaker that you are interested in their idea and are seeking more information about it. It gives the speaker an opportunity to go into greater detail, which will increase the listener's understanding of the message.

Clarifying is a different type of question that doesn't seek more information but rather a clearing up of any possible confusion or meaning. An example of a clarifying question is 'When you mentioned reducing costs, what exactly did you mean?' This type of question gives the speaker the opportunity to state their message in a different way that is more clear to the listener. In this case, the speaker would give a concrete example of what types of expenditures need to be reduced.

Reflection

As an active listener, you can also use reflection to show signs of being attentive to the speaker's message. In this situation, you restate the message and emotion of the speaker using your own words. Like a mirror, this sign reflects back to the speaker a version of their message that they can then confirm the accuracy of or correct any errors in the communication.

Reflection is a way for you to see if you are getting an accurate picture of the emotion of the speaker's message. Imagine you're listening to a friend telling you about how much work they had to do. They rattle off a long list of tasks followed by a litany of errands they ran after work. Then they finish with what they still need to complete before going to bed.

Using reflection, you would say something like, 'wow, you must be feeling worn out after getting so much done.' This statement reflects back to the speaker how they must be feeling after having a full plate of responsibilities. It also gives an indication of your attentiveness to their emotional state when you reflect on the feelings you perceived from the message.

Summarization

An ability to provide a summarization is the final verbal sign that you received the speaker's message accurately. As an active listener, you should be able to give a condensed synopsis of the speaker's message that expresses the meaning and the emotion. Using your own words and phrasing, an active listener can accurately encapsulate the full message of the speaker.

When you use summarization, you are essentially going through the entire message and reporting back to the speaker the main points. Your goal is to ensure you have heard all of the important components of the message. In addition, when you use summarization, you are confirming with the speaker that you have a full understanding of the message as a whole.

Styles of Communication for Active Listening

Being an active listener requires the ability to use a variety of communication styles to ensure you perceived the message correctly. These different types of conversation tools work towards the same goal of coming to a mutual understanding. These methods of conveyance help you, the active listener, to confirm the meaning of the message. They also help the speaker to evaluate how well their message is being understood.

Paraphrasing

Paraphrasing is one style in which you can communicate how well you are understanding what the speaker is saying. When you paraphrase someone's message, the goal is to say it in another way while preserving the intended meaning. For instance, the boss calls you into the office for an informal review of your performance. He is displeased by your sudden decline in productivity and the increase in your tardiness. He explains this behavior is unacceptable and expects to see an improvement immediately.

To assure your boss the message was received you tell your boss, 'I understand you are unhappy with my lapse in punctuality and the quality of my work. You have high expectations that are not unattainable if I do my best.' This restating of the essence of the boss's message shows him you understand what the problem is, how he feels about it, and what needs to be done to fix the situation.

Reflecting Feeling

The next two styles of communication use reflection and paraphrasing in the form of a question to better understand the speaker's message. An active listener will reflect the feeling of the speaker's words by asking a question as it relates to the speaker's mood. For example, you might say 'You sound frustrated about how you were given more assignments.'

Reflection of the speaker's feelings helps to create a rapport on an emotional level. It builds a connection between the speaker and the listener where the mutual focus is accurately identifying the feeling of the message. It is important that you be sure not to confuse how a person feels emotionally with passing judgment on them. Sadness is an emotional feeling while laziness is a judgment of character.

Reflecting Meaning

As an active listener, you can also use a reflection of the speaker's meaning to confirm understanding of the message. Put in the form of a question to seek clarity, the attentive listener states facts about the message, not feelings, to assess meaning. For example, you might say to your boss, 'My tardiness has slowed down production for the whole team, is that what you're saying?'

Reflection of meaning takes out the emotional connection of the message to focus on the specific actions. This type of clarification keeps the focus away from feelings and looks to address the concrete problem-- in this case, your tardiness. Reflecting on the meaning helps to minimize feelings of being attacked by looking at the factual information.

Summative Reflection

Summative reflection combines both the reflection of feeling and reflection of meaning to get full confirmation the listener received the message correctly. As an active listener, you can use both styles of reflection in combination to clarify the speaker's feelings and meaning. In this full summarization, the attentive active listener will have all of the pieces of the puzzle put properly in place giving a clear and complete picture.

The 13 Blocks to Active Listening

Communication requires an equal share of self-expression and active listening. As the listener, we have to be aware of the forms of expression that block our ability to actively listen. Before you can learn to use the right tools, you must rid yourself of the wrong tools. These 13 blocks to active listening are the reason we fail to listen most effectively.

1. Mind Reading

When you think you know someone well, you get the idea that you know exactly what they are thinking. You're listening to them speak and you become focused on what you think they're going to say next. You may even jump in and finish their sentence for them since you're so sure of your mind-reading skills.

Mind reading may be a great stage performance act but when you're the speaker being interrupted by a sentence finisher, the show stops. When you become so focused on predicting the message, you risk missing an important part of the real message. In addition, if you're completely off the mark, you've just derailed the conversation and quite possibly embarrassed yourself.

2. Rehearsing

Like an actor waiting in the wing, the rehearser practices what they are going to say when the speaker is finished talking. The problem with this block is the lack of attentiveness the listener is giving the speaker. When rehearsing, you have a prewritten script in mind that guides your interaction but the speaker may be 'reading' from a different script. This incongruence in dialogue is the result of practicing an answer without even knowing the question being asked.

Rehearsing is best left for when you have to give a speech, not when you're in the midst of a conversation. Give the speaker your full attention. Take time to absorb their message, not the one you created in your mind, and then respond with forethought. When you try to drive the conversation with your script instead of experiencing the conversation in real-time, you'll soon find yourself alone on that dim stage.

3. Filtering

Also referred to as selective listening, someone using filtering is only paying attention to what they want to hear. People who use filtering are often searching the message for clues of danger. It's a self-preservation instinct we use to detect a threat from others. You become so focused on their emotional level that you become distracted from the message.

Filtering blocks you from getting the entire message when you're only tuned into keywords. Meaning can change drastically when you miss a word or two. Your teen comes home a few minutes late and tells you 'Sorry, I'm late. I dropped off a friend after I filled up the gas tank so you won't have to get up so early to get gas in the morning.'

You being already upset at typical teenage tardiness, all you keyed in on were dropping off a friend and having to get up early to get gas. You missed the most important part-- the gem of a good deed that your teen did for you. You were expecting bad news from a curfew violator and heard what you wanted to hear, missing the message entirely.

4. Judging

We're told not to judge a book by its cover. Then of course there's the book that tells us not to judge others because then they might judge us. But try as we might, we stumble on this block of judging occasionally in conversation. Judging during communication occurs when you have a predetermined attitude about the message based on your opinion of the speaker.

Judging can occur when the boss assigns you to work on a committee with a co-worker you like and one, not so much. When you have a negative opinion of someone, you prejudge any ideas they may have as being terrible. And in the reverse, when you have a positive opinion of the person, you are more likely to judge their ideas more positively. In reality, good ideas and bad ideas can come from anyone so listen to everyone before you decide.

5. Daydreaming

Daydreaming happens to the best of us. You're listening to someone tell a story and a word or phrase triggers a memory. Perhaps it's the name of a song and now you start thinking about the last time you heard that tune. Before you know it, you have completely disconnected from the conversation and you have no idea what the other person just said.

This block illustrates how active our brains are and how much effort we must exert to stay focused in the now. Daydreaming can happen for a number of other reasons including boredom or lack of interest. Staying focused when the speaker is going on and on about something uninteresting can certainly lead to daydreaming and missing the message.

6. Advising

One of the most common blocks to interpersonal communication is when the listener becomes the adviser. This happens when one person is in need of expressing themselves and the listener mistakes the message for a cry of help. You just want to vent about that speeding ticket you didn't deserve or the ridiculous prices at that new restaurant. In sweeps the adviser with suggestions of 'drive slower next time' and 'high quality does cost more so what did you expect?'

Advising may sound like a good idea and that you're being helpful, but unless they asked you for advice, it's typically unwanted. The speaker just wants to share their thoughts and feelings with you, but you incorrectly repay their openness with 'here's what you should have done' or 'next time I would...'. An active listener's role is to comprehend the message of the speaker whereas advising is an attempt to define the message.

7. Sparring

Sometimes called boxing, this active listening block is an aggressive and argumentative stance against the speaker and their message. You jab at the speaker with snap judgments turning the conversation into a competition. The speaker feels they are not being listened to and becomes defensive when you have them back into the corner from your attacks.

It's normal to not always agree on things but that doesn't mean it has to become an argument. The use of sparring is an intentional attack on the other person. The focus is no longer on the speaker but on your mission to convince them your view is better. If your partner is saying things like 'that isn't what I'm saying' or 'you're just not understanding me', you may be sparring instead of listening.

8. Being Right

This block to active listening happens when you believe there is no possible way you could be wrong. Oftentimes these are people who need to have the last word. They will pull out all the stops to ensure you know they are right. When challenged, the "I am right" communicator will resort to aggressive tactics.

Needing to be right when you're being proven wrong leads you to attack the other person instead of recognizing the wrong. You offend them with name-calling or you criticize them to put them on the defense. If you find it difficult to hear corrective criticism from others, your listening may be blocked by the need to be right.

9. Derailing

Derailing is a tactic used by listeners who don't want to hear the message of the speaker. You disrupt the speaker's flow of communication with interjections and subject changes. The goal of the derailer is to avoid addressing the issue brought forth by the messenger. You throw out distractions or dodge the speaker to keep from staying on track.

An unwillingness to communicate about a subject will snowball into more problems in the relationship. Trying to derail a conversation happens when someone isn't ready to face the situation and they may need time to be open to listening. If someone is using derailing to avoid a subject of discussion give them the opportunity to come back to it when they're more prepared.

10. Placating

If you find yourself agreeing with everything the other person is saying, even when you don't really agree, you are placating them. When you agree too quickly in an attempt to please the speaker rather than a genuine agreement, your focus is in the wrong place. Being an active listener is about support and understanding.

More importantly, attentive active listening is about seeing the value of the messenger and their message. If you're more concerned with whether or not you agree with the speaker instead of learning who the speaker is and how they feel, you'll struggle with building genuine relationships. Being surrounded by people who agree with everything you say will become tiresome and dull. Life's much more exciting when we have different ideas.

11. Comparing

The need to gauge who is better or smarter during a conversation is known as comparing. When you engage in this type of blocking, it is often the result of low self-esteem or devalued self-worth. An active listener who is confident in themselves will be able to listen to others and see them as uniquely valuable.

Basing your self-worth by comparing yourself to others is an unhealthy and inaccurate form of measurement. We each have different experiences and opportunities that influence where we are in life. When you are able to see your own worth and value to others, you won't feel the need to compare your life experiences to others.

12. Identifying

Sometimes when we are trying to build rapport with someone we use identifying to show them we understand. These are the "oh, me too" stories told to let the speaker know we know exactly what they're talking about. We jump in to share in an attempt to communicate a common bond.

Unfortunately, what occurs with identifying is a change in focus from the speaker's experience to yours. While having a common experience is helpful to understanding each other, interjecting your story in mid-talk is disruptive and rude. Essentially, identifying in this context is a potential derailing as well.

13. Dismissing

The last block that prevents actively listening to the speaker is known as dismissing. You're using this block if you make statements that devalue the speaker's feelings. Telling someone 'it's not that big of a deal' or that they need to 'just forget about it' disregards the feelings of the speaker. And if you are not able to respect how they feel, how can they believe you respect them as a person?

When you're dismissive of their message, you are telling the speaker what they're saying has no value and thus unworthy of being heard. If we are to expect others to be willing to listen to our needs, fears, or frustrations, we first must be open to hearing theirs. We each have strengths and weaknesses and it is up to each of us to pull others up. Dismissing their experience tells them you see them as weak or unworthy.

Active Listening Enhancers

By removing all of the blocks to active listening you clear the way for using the tools that enhance active listening. Your efforts to do all you can to effectively listen to the other person will go a long way toward building rapport. In order to fully appreciate the power of listening, you need to understand how these enhancers work.

Strong Eye Contact and Full Attention

Mastering the art of strong eye contact that exhibits focus and attentiveness without becoming an awkward staring contest will get easier with practice. You can only obtain strong eye contact by facing the speaker when they are talking. If you're looking around the room or staring into your computer screen, your attention to the speaker is sporadic. And for them, your focus is a moving target they can't seem to connect with directly.

Looking the speaker in the eye shows them you are being attentive to them. It shows them you're engaged in the conversation and taking notice of them fully. You're also more inclined to pick up the subtle non-verbal clues from their facial expression when you are giving the speaker your full attention.

Maintain Silence While Listening

Learning to have patience and be able to wait until the speaker is finished before you speak takes willpower. It also shows respect to the speaker when you don't interrupt them. Remaining quiet while they speak shows that you feel what they have to say is important. You also show them through your respectful silence that you care about their opinion and how they feel.

You must also refrain from trying to finish the speaker's sentences or filling in the pauses when they seem stuck. Give them the opportunity to take the time they need to convey their message to you. When you interject your thoughts into their message, you risk being wrong which will certainly derail the conversation. Be patient. Let them finish what they need to say their way and at their pace.

Withholding Judgment

Keeping an open-mind by not passing judgment on the speaker or the message displays your level of maturity. It also reflects to the speaker you're willing to examine and evaluate the message on its own merit. It shows them you are accommodating to their perspective and understand their point of view.

As an active listener, you must keep your mind clear of preconceived opinions or judgments about the speaker or their message. When you convict the messenger based on your beliefs, you have ceased to listen. Furthermore, the messenger will be less likely to communicate openly with you in the future, which in turn, will cause your relationship to deteriorate.

Asking for More Information

As an active listener, you should ask questions to show the speaker you want to understand and you are striving to be empathic to their situation. When you take time to ask follow-up questions you are able to gain more information about the message. You are also giving the speaker a clear indication you are invested in the conversation.

Your questions will help the speaker to elaborate on what happened, how it made them feel, or what would make things better. Asking for more information is a great way for you to get the speaker thinking about the message they're telling and dig deeper towards a solution. Your questions will help the speaker to elaborate on the matter at hand and give them new insights they hadn't considered.

Commitment to Problem Solving

You have a responsibility as an active listener to take the required actions that will resolve the speaker's situation. Being the greatest active listener will require you to do more than just hear the cry for help or the discord of frustration. You must make a commitment to address the speaker's concerns and change your own behaviors that are negatively impacting resolve.

As an active listener, your job is to build a stronger connection with the people in your lives. To do so, requires you to have the knowledge of the problem and the desire to do something about it. We all find times in our lives where we need help but are afraid to ask. Be the one people can count on when life gets to be too much.

Chapter 2 Recap

★ Active listening is a commitment to communicate at a level that shows respect to each other. It requires self-discipline to focus our thoughts on someone else.

★ Active listening incorporates both the spoken word and the non-verbal manners in which we speak. It is important to pay attention to all aspects of the message, which includes the physicality of active listening and the ways in which we converse.

★ Blocks to our ability to actively listen must first be recognized in order to get rid of them. They have been used as a shield in an attempt at self-preservation. Once removed the ability to hear each other will be much easier.

★ Using positive active listening enhancers will help you to stop using communication blocks and encourage relationships to flourish. Learning to value one another begins when we have learned how to value ourselves.

★ Learning how to be an active listener asks you to evaluate your own faults and be willing to work on being a better you.

Chapter 3: The Power of Empathy

Do you find that you have an instinct that detects how others are feeling? Are you often able to tell when someone is being dishonest? Maybe you're the one everyone comes to when they have a problem, the genuinely caring friend or co-worker. If you're the kind of person who tends to the well-being of others and takes action to help when they're in need, then you are familiar with empathy.

Empathy is the deeper connection you feel from sharing the mood and understanding of another's experience through their eyes. When you are empathic, you put aside your own bias and worldview to see the situation from their mindset. You have a sensitivity to identify the emotions of the speaker and are able to experience their problem vicariously.

With empathy, you are able to connect with others in both thought and feelings. You possess compassion and regard for other people's needs. Empathy is the desire to pursue the motivations and emotions underneath the spoken word of the message. It is a willingness to ask follow-up questions to clear up any confusion you may have or ambiguities in the meaning.

When you are empathic, you take time to meet the needs of others when they are struggling. Your consideration for others well-being creates a sense of safety and security in your relationships. Empathy gives you the power to build a solid foundation for solving problems by getting to the root of behaviors that are creating conflict.

Empathy requires you to be comfortable with those moments of silence when the speaker has paused to collect their thoughts. Perhaps they need to gather their composure before they're able to continue. Your ability to stay quiet must remain strong, allowing them to take the time they need to express themselves completely.

Types of Empathy

Most of us don't experience empathy in the same way. There are even some people who seem to possess little to no empathy at all. If you lack empathy, it creates a barrier in your relationships that prevents you from completely knowing the other person. You feel disconnected and emotionally distant because you don't understand how the other person is thinking or feeling.

Fortunately, most people you encounter in your life are a healthy mix of the three different types of empathy; cognitive, affective, and somatic.

Cognitive Empathy

You are cognitively empathic if you are able to understand the other person's way of thinking. You understand their mindset because you know where their ideas are coming from. With cognitive empathy, you are able to comprehend their belief system because you're familiar with what they have been through.

Cognitive empathy is focused on what the other person is thinking and how they perceive the situation or conflict. You are able to get into their head and see how they see the world and understand thoughts from their point of view.

Affective Empathy

When you understand the emotions the other person is expressing, you are experiencing affective empathy. You are able to sense their sadness or fear because you relate to their struggle. Your ability to discern their mood from their message is what helps you to appropriately respond to the situation.

Affective empathy occurs when you are able to step into the other person's shoes to feel the same way they do. You can understand why they are angry or frustrated because you too feel as they do about the conflict. This emotional connection you have as an affective-empathic leads the way for compassionate actions for the well-being of others.

Somatic Empathy

If you have ever experienced a physical reaction related to the emotional display of the other person, you have somatic empathy. You are the type who blushes alongside the embarrassed classmate when she forgets her line on opening night. Or maybe you're the one who tears up when someone you love is feeling broken-hearted.

Somatic empathy occurs when your body reacts in a physical manner to the emotions of another person. Have you ever grimaced in pain when you saw someone else get punched? Perhaps you are the kind of person who gets an upset stomach when their teammate is feeling nervous about the big game. Researchers believe this physical response to other's feelings is connected to the neurons that enable you to mirror someone else's mood.

Empathy Barriers

In addition to the three types of empathy you may experience, there are three barriers that can prevent you from feeling empathic. Each of these empathy blockers is an internal belief you may hold that will obstruct you from accurately assessing the situation. Only after clearing your mind of these misguided notions will you be able to correctly understand the people and the world around you.

Cognitive Bias

Your perception of the world, such as what's right versus what's wrong, influences how you interact with others. Likewise, your beliefs and opinions about the people you engage with affect how you communicate with them. Your thinking, or cognitive bias, can be an inhibitor to empathic understanding of the other person. And without an understanding, you will struggle to relate to them and their situation.

An example of a cognitive bias is when you believe the reason other people fail is because of who they are as a person while your own failures are because of external circumstances. Your flawed thinking tells you the reason Larry forgot his laptop's power cord again is because he's a forgetful klutz. But what if it turned out that Larry has a toddler at home who snuck into daddy's work bag to find the candy he hides for him? Quite possibly the little guy snatched the cord pretending it was a toy. This paints a whole different picture of Larry now, doesn't it?

Dehumanization

When you are unable to relate to the other person's situation, the misconception of dehumanizing may step in to block your ability to be empathic. You believe that your experience is much different than their experience because you live in different worlds. For example, you feel less empathy towards a celebrity whose house was robbed than you do for your neighbor whose car was stolen.

You don't feel as bad for them as you do your neighbor because the celebrity is rich and famous and can just buy new stuff. You dismiss their feelings of loss and privacy invasion because they're not like 'regular people', right? They don't feel the same pain we do, do they? Of course, they probably have better insurance but they do feel human feelings too. We are, for the most part, all human and should treat each other equally when empathy is a factor.

Another example of when you may lack empathy due to dehumanization is when tragedy strikes in a foreign country versus close to home. It's difficult for most people to relate to the conditions of poor nations if you haven't seen it first hand. So when you see flooding in a country you've never heard of you may shrug it off as 'they're probably used to it.' But when Hurricanes Katrina and Harvey pounded the Gulf Coast with a deluge of rains, your empathy probably kicked in if you have family or friends who live there.

Victim-Blaming

By far the most heinous of the three empathy barriers, victim-blaming happens far too often in the modern world. As a victim-blamer, you believe that the person must have done something to deserve the tragedy that befell them. You conclude that their suffering is justified because they were asking for it. Surely the victim must have provoked the attacker in some way, right?

Victim-blaming prevents you from believing the other person's experience. It puts doubt in your mind because you've already passed judgment on them. You look for proof in their message to corroborate the narrative in your own mind. As a victim-blamer, you are unable to relate to their situation because you would have never done this or that as they did.

When you blame the victim for their suffering, you strip them of their dignity and you absolve the attacker of wrongful behavior in one snap. Empathy is a skill that we all need to build stronger connections with everyone we encounter. By building each other up with solidarity and regard, you can help get rid of the flawed belief of victim-blaming.

Why be empathic?

If you want to construct healthy social connections with the people in your life, be it at work or in your home, you need the power of empathy. When you understand the thinking and the emotion of the other person, you are better equipped to respond to the social situation appropriately. You are able to assess their needs and take action to help them resolve the conflict.

Your empathy builds trust in your relationships by showing them you have respect for how they think and feel. It encourages the people in your life to be open and honest in their communication when they know you listen with an empathic heart and mind. Being an empathic listener means you provide a secure, stress-reducing, safe zone for emotional expression, free of judgment.

Empathy begets happiness for the person you help and for you as well. Making the world a better place can literally begin with the compassion of one person. Imagine how great life could be if we took time to put a smile on someone else's face. Building positive social connections is a vital component of your overall health and well-being. Being harmonious with the world around you and the people you encounter directly affects your emotional health. And when your mental well-being is put into jeopardy, it's only a matter of time before your physical health begins to suffer.

Your empathy gives acknowledgment of the speaker and establishes their importance to you. It builds confidence in the speaker's self-esteem when you truly listen to understand them as a person. When you are empathic you are able to develop open and honest relationships because you respect the other person's thoughts and feelings. Together you are able to explore the situation deeper by addressing questions that seek to solve the problem. And gaining cooperation leads to stronger bonds.

Mastering the skills of empathy will help you to monitor your own emotional responses to situations and people. Being aware of how others respond to you during encounters will help you to gauge how well or poorly you are expressing yourself. If you are doing well at keeping your own feelings in-check, you will find people want to be around you. If however, you find yourself watching others storming off in anger or frustration, you need to assess your empathy skills and make a change.

When you use empathy to build relationships, you create a foundation of integrity and reverence. It makes you a better, more considerate individual when you can set aside your life for a moment to make a world of a difference in someone else's. By developing better communication through greater empathic understanding, you will foster higher levels of productivity from co-workers. You'll also have high-quality relationships with family and friends when you harness the power of empathy.

How to be an Empathic Listener

Your goal as an empathic listener is to see the conversation from the speaker's mindset. To do this you must step outside of your own feelings and cognitive bias to evaluate the situation in their shoes. When you allow yourself to fully experience their cognitive and emotional perspective, it comes with the risk of feeling personal pain. As an empathic listener, you will see yourself through their eyes and we don't always like what we see.

In order to become more empathic to the diversity of the human spirit, you must experience the variety of life that is unfamiliar. Travel and see what it's really like to walk a mile in someone else's reality. Volunteer at a shelter to connect with people to better understand the struggles of homelessness if you want to increase your empathic compassion for others. Be the example of positive energy that shines a beacon of hope to someone who may feel lost and alone.

During this learning excursion of life experience, you will have the opportunity to get to know yourself completely. To be an effective empathic listener you must first understand how your experiences have influenced your way of thinking. More importantly, you must address those misconceptions that are impairing your ability to listen with compassion.

Show your empathy and compassion through actions by treating them as you would want them to treat you. Give a smile of encouragement as you pay full attention to the conversation to show you are listening. And listen with both an open-mind and a caring heart giving full regard to their body language and tone of voice. Reflect back to identify what they are thinking and feeling to ensure you are not confusing your own thoughts and emotions as theirs.

Stages of Empathic Listening

Every new skill requires practice in order to become more proficient. You wouldn't go on stage in a grand concert hall without playing the piano every day to ensure your performance goes well. That being said, the only way you can expect to be the most effective listener is through daily practice.

Stage 1

Empathy skills start with baby steps at their basic level. At this stage of listening, you use their words when repeating back what you heard in the message. If they say, 'I'm angry at the way you handled the situation', you would say, "I understand you are angry.'

Stage 1 is about being exact to their word and not trying to put your own spin on the situation. You use their word 'angry' and listen to understand what they mean by it. When first learning about someone else, you should stick with repeating back exact phrasing until you understand the person's precise or understated meaning. For some, 'angry' means they feel frustrated, while for others it may indicate a much stronger emotion. Until you are more familiar with the speaker, stick with the exact words they chose.

Stage 2

Once you begin to build rapport with the other person, your empathic listening will move up to stage 2. By now, you have gotten to know the other person a little better with a clearer picture of who they are as a person. You have conversed on a number of occasions giving you more clues to their thinking and mood. Your conversations have given you insight into their word choice and meaning, as well as, non-verbal cues.

Stage 2 uses paraphrasing of the speaker's message rather than parroting back their message word for word. Here you are able to use your own familiar terms to verbalize your understanding of the message they are trying to convey. You are expressing to them you understand the facts they have presented and you add nothing more.

If they were to say 'I hate when my daughter slams her door when I'm trying to talk to her.' At stage 2 listening, you might respond with, 'I understand that your daughter's slamming the door really upsets you'. You have stated back the facts of the message in your own phrasing that confirms understanding without making any judgment calls on the situation.

Stage 3

This next stage of empathic listening is reached when you have become more in tune with the people around you. You have taken the time to pay attention and get to know the person you are conversing with to better understand them. You are at the stage when you can tell something's wrong with a friend or colleague before they've even come to you for help.

At this level of listening, you reflect back on the emotion you have detected from their message. You show them you understand how they feel in your own words. For example, your friend tells you her significant other has been avoiding an issue. You can tell by her tone and body language she's worried. You respond to her empathically by saying, 'you seem worried about the lack of communication in your relationship.' You reflect the feeling you sense they are experiencing in order to confirm or correct your interpretation.

Stage 3 empathic listening means you have actively worked on improving your interpersonal communication. It shows the people in your life that you value their feelings and are respectful of their point of view, even when it differs from your own. Genuine empathic listening requires you to put someone else's needs ahead of your own. Then when you find yourself in a time of need, you're more apt to find someone who will throw you a line.

Stage 4
The final stage of empathy is reached when you are able to reflect back to the speaker both the feeling and the meaning of their message. You will be able to read the emotions of the people in your life much more clearly at this stage. Combined with your continued interactions and gaining of understanding of their perspective, you are better able to meet others' needs.

Empathic listening is a skill that builds upon itself the more you work on honing your instincts of compassion. This highest level of empathy shows others you are both in command of your own feelings and strong enough to guide others through life. It reveals to the people in your life that you value others as they are and have committed to being a positive impact on humanity.

Chapter 3 Recap

★ Empathy is a moment of selfless sacrifice where you set aside personal comfort for the sake of helping another human being. You are empathic if you take the time to do something for someone else without expectations of accolades or compensation.

★ Being an empathic listener requires you to be mindful and present in the conversation. It takes a caring spirit to be able to identify someone else's pains and struggles. Empathy also requires wisdom to examine the logic in conjunction with the emotion.

★ We each experience life in our own way and the same holds true for your way of experiencing empathy. You can have a range of empathic skill levels from the three types; the emotions of affective, the thoughts from cognitive empathy, or the physical manifestations of somatic empathy.

★ True empathic listening can only be achieved after you recognize and rid your mindset of the three barriers of empathy: cognitive bias when our thoughts get in the way, dehumanization where we don't see their situation as comparative to you own, and victim-blaming where you see the person as being deserving of the misfortune.

★ Empathy is a skill that can transfer from one person to another. When you become more empathic to the needs of others, they will emulate your actions to become more empathic as well. Relationships at work and at home will benefit from your empathic nature, which improves everyone's quality of life.

★ Effective empathic listening builds stronger over time. You must actively work towards being your best if you are to be good at what you do. Taking steps to increase your stage of listening requires commitment but is worth the effort.

★ Each stage of empathic listening you are able to master will increase your overall chances of reaching the highest level of compassion and understanding in your relationships. Our connective nature flourishes when we each take part in living life.

Our purpose in life is not just simply to exist. You and I have a spirit that craves experience and a connection to the world and the people around us. We have minds that hunger for knowledge and an understanding of the life we experience and why it differs for others. And each one of us has a heart filled with fears and desires that needs a shining light of empathic encouragement from one another to make all of our lives glow a little brighter.

Chapter 4 Speaking with Empathy

Have you ever found yourself at a loss for words after a friend has revealed a struggle they are experiencing at home? Or perhaps a co-worker has confided in you the battle they are having with a project at work? Does it ever seem like you just don't know what to say to help the friend or co-worker feel better? You may not have all the answers they need, but by learning how to speak with empathy, you can offer support that is both effective and compassionate.

Your choice of words when responding to someone in need plays a crucial role in learning to speak empathically. You will find that with continued practice of all the skills you have learned thus far, mastering the vocabulary of empathic responses will become easier. Speaking with empathy isn't about memorizing lines from a script like you would in a play. It's about exerting the effort needed to learn what it means to respond with empathy, whatever the situation.

Empathy has a goal of your attunement to the other person's situation. You are not being effectively empathic by simply parroting back words in a feeble attempt to understand the speaker's message. You must immerse yourself in their experience before you'll be able to know and feel the situation as the other person does. You will have a clearer idea of what to say to the other person when you make the effort to be in their shoes. What would you want someone to say to you when facing the same situation?

Your empathic communication should be a process of affirmation. It creatively expresses your acceptance of the other person and their message.

You show the other person a desire to genuinely understand how they think and feel when you listen and speak with empathy. When you learn to speak with empathy, your communication skills will continue to improve leading to the development of better relationships.

Real empathy requires you to be fully attentive to the conversation. You must be completely present emotionally and intellectually. Your mind has a tendency to focus on your own problems and feelings. Even when you care about the other person and offer a listening ear, empathic communication requires your dedicated concentration.

It takes forgetting about yourself and your own conflicts to give your undivided attention to the other person. You have to take control of your own thoughts and dedicate your cognitive focus to the person in need of your help. Good intentions will only go so far when you're trying to be there for someone in need. Real understanding is shown when you take part in making a difference that will have a positive impact on both the conflict and your relationship with the person you're helping.

When you are inattentive and thinking of yourself, you minimize the other person's value to you in their eyes. Your lack of paying attention gives the other person the impression what they're saying isn't important enough to keep you engaged. Being disconnected empathically from the people in your life will lead to hurt feelings and damaged relationships.

Being able to fully communicate your empathy requires a desire to pause your own life for just a moment. Take time out to actively listen to the other person and fully engage in the conversation. Most importantly, your choice of words must speak in a manner that conveys both clear understanding and purposefulness. At the highest level of empathy, you will find yourself moved to take action to help when someone is in need.

Your empathic response comes from a combination of a kind heart and an open mind. You must be able to fully commit your time and attentiveness to the conversation. You have to let go of your own feelings about the other person's situation. You take in the conflict from the perspective of the speaker in order to fully appreciate their plight and how it is affecting them.

Empathic response requires that you let go of your judgments and bias. Resist the desire to make suggestions or give helpful advice. When you speak with empathic responses, you confirm with the other person they have been heard. Compassionate empathic communication occurs when your focus is on being an encouragement to someone when the burdens of their life weigh too heavy.

When you give of yourself in a genuine manner, you build stronger interpersonal relationships created from trust, respect, and human decency. By taking the time to be in the moment for someone and hold their burden with them, you provide comfort to that person. You give them encouragement when they know you're someone they can count on.

Types of Empathic Responses

Your ability to respond empathically will emerge as you master the habits of listening empathically. You will find that the right words will come to you more naturally when you've actively listened and taken notice of nonverbal cues. Knowing to pause for a moment as you digest the message is critical before asking clarifying questions.

Speaking with empathy is also about using words that signify teamwork. Your empathic language will use the terms 'we' and 'us' instead of 'me' and 'you'. 'We'll get through this together,' is much more comforting and compassionate to someone feeling alone than to tell them 'You're going to be fine' or 'that happened to me once.'

The three types of empathic responses available to you serve a specific purpose and should be used where best suited. Each of the three types gives you a better perspective of the speaker's conflict in need of resolve. One type, cognitive, looks at the problem from the eye of the intellect. The second type is emotional and sees the scene from the eye of the heart. When you combine the strengths of both, you will harness the life-changing power of compassionate response.

Cognitive Empathic Response

You're expressing a cognitive empathic response when your focus is knowing what the other person is thinking with regard to their situation. You are looking at the problem from a logical perspective as to why the person is feeling as they do. Your focus is on the logic and reasoning of the conflict the person is experiencing. It is an intellectual understanding of the dilemma through facts.

Your cognitive empathic response occurs when you have the ability to rationalize the situation and comprehend why the person feels the way they do. You use this type of response in work relationships and situations involving intellectual discussions. It's highly effective for times when you are in a negotiation.

Your cognitive empathic response is also essential for you to be able to work effectively with a diverse population. You will find it much easier to guide a group towards a common goal when you possess their understanding at a cognitive level. You are examining the situation from an intellectual realm that lets go of any personal emotional attachments that could cloud your perspective of the issue.

Speaking with your cognitive empathic response does not address the feelings associated with the conflict. As such, it can cause a disconnect from the person's emotional state and block you from fully understanding what they are going through. Relying only on your logical understanding without feeling the emotional impact of the situation doesn't give you the complete picture.

Emotional Empathic Response

Your emotional empathic response occurs when you are able to recognize and experience the emotions of the other person. You use this type of response most often for personal relationships with family and close friends. You also express this type of empathic response in career fields where empathy is essential to the job. This includes such professions as health and hospice care or jobs that involve daily living skills such as education and special care.

Expressing an emotional empathic response comes from understanding how the other person feels on an emotional level. You experience first-hand the feelings they are expressing to you. Your empathic response is at the physical level being influenced by your brain's mirror neurons, emulating the feelings you see before you.

You're connecting with the other person on a molecular level when you experience emotional empathic communication. You gain new insight from feeling their fear or their frustration that may differ from how you experience those emotions. In times when feelings play a key role in the relationship, harnessing your empathic response will encourage conversation and strengthen bonds.

You may find that getting emotionally engaged in an effort to help others will take its toll on your personal strength and mental well-being. That's why it is important to not overextend yourself to the point of exhaustion. You can't expect to effectively assist the people in your life when you failed to first take care of your own well-being.

Compassionate Empathic Response

The highest level of empathic response you can achieve is the compassionate empathic response that moves you to take action. You become a compassionate empath when you set aside your own needs and take an active role in helping someone who is struggling. You will be able to create the strongest interpersonal bonds when you engage in a compassionate empathic response.

When you are able to combine the intellect of cognitive empathy with the physical experience of emotional empathy you are more inclined to reach the level of compassion people need from one another. You will find that having genuine compassion for the people in your life will move you in a way that inspires you to be a part of helping conquer the battles of others.

Compassionate empathic response requires you to have both the intellectual comprehension of the situation and knowledge of what would be helpful to the other person. You must also possess a sensitivity to emotional awareness of the person to properly assess how your actions will affect how they feel. Compassionate empathy helps you to take into account all aspects of the human experience by acknowledging how and why we think and feel as we do.

What Not to Say

You may find it hard to know what to say when just starting your journey of empathic response. But with practice, you will get better. Your first goal is to rid yourself of the old cliches and well-worn phrases you've probably heard time and time again. 'It will all come out in the wash', 'She's not hurting anymore,' and of course, 'Things always happen for a reason.'

Using these kinds of empty phrases gives the other person no sense of your understanding their pain or struggle. Telling someone to 'look at it as a blessing' or 'it could be worse' ignores the person's perception of the conflict and minimizes their feelings. Did it ever make you feel better to hear someone tell you 'you'll get over it' or 'it just wasn't meant to be?'

Speak with Cognitive Empathy

Using statements that show you acknowledge what the person is going through tells them that you understand their thinking. Phrases such as 'That must have been difficult for you,' or 'I can understand why you are having trouble' let the other person know it's logical for them to feel as they do. You are assuring them of a mutual understanding of the conflict.

You can also use cognitive empathic responses to indicate you are interested in helping them and are grateful for their open and honest communication. Show them you appreciate their input with statements like 'Thank you for bringing this to my attention,' and 'I value your opinion on this matter.' By using words of encouragement that address the other person's way of thinking, you help to lower their shields of defense caused by feelings of inadequacy.

For example, your co-worker tells you they are thinking about quitting because of the new policy enacted at work. They go on to explain how they view what this change will do to the morale of the team. You know how much they enjoy their job and how much they contribute to the team. How should you respond to show your co-worker you understand how they are thinking?

When using a cognitive empathic response, your words should focus on how the person is thinking in relation to the new policy. You can express your cognitive understanding of the situation by saying, 'I understand this new policy has concerned you enough to consider leaving a job you enjoy and do so well. I know how hard you work and how much you contribute to the team.'

With this type of response, you convey that you understand the logical reason they have presented for wanting to quit. Your level of rapport with the person will guide your words of encouragement. In this example, giving praise to how much they mean to you and others on the team instills confidence. When someone believes in you, you believe in yourself more.

It also shows them you are an ally that appreciates their honesty about the situation. It lets them know they can talk to you as they work through their battle. Your cognitive empathy addresses the thought process of decision-making without letting emotions cloud up the right or wrong of what to do next. You assure the person they have reasoning behind their choice and not just some knee-jerk reaction to an unexpected change on the job.

You could also use cognitive empathic responses when a friend tells you about what a lousy job the mechanic did fixing their car. You can see that your friend is angry at being ripped off, and understandably so. You know how expensive car repairs can be. In this instance, using a cognitive empathic response is sufficient for conveying your understanding of why they are upset.

By saying, 'You're right to be upset. There's a certain level of expectation in quality of service at those rates,' you give your friend confirmation that you are in agreeance. You are telling them you are aligned with their logical reaction to the situation and are accepting of their expression of anger. Through careful word choice, you can express your cognitive empathy and acknowledge their feelings without needing to feel the anger for yourself.

Speak with Emotional Empathy

Responding appropriately to someone using emotional empathic response is a more delicate procedure than the use of cognitive empathy. Using phrases like 'that must have been painful' or 'my heart aches knowing that happened' tells them you are hurting with them. Let them know you feel honored by their trust in you with statements like, 'it takes courage to share how you're feeling.'

And don't be afraid to admit when you're not sure how they are feeling by saying things like 'I'm at a loss for words,' or simply ask them, 'how did that make you feel?' It is much better to admit you're unsure and let them clarify than to try and guess when you're not certain. As you get to know people better, you will be able to more accurately gauge their emotional level.

To illustrate this type of empathic response more clearly, imagine your teenager has just come home from school with their first broken heart. You can see they are upset, maybe even a bit angry at what has transpired. You remember what young love was like and how much it hurts the first time it crashes to an abrupt end.

Your response focuses on the emotions your teenager is feeling and giving them assurance that how they are feeling is valid. You could say, 'I know you're hurting right now. You're a loving and caring individual and how you're feeling right now is expected.' Emotional empathic responses are intended to show the other person you feel their pain too because what they are experiencing is a natural part of life and relationships.

Your goal with emotional empathic communication isn't about changing how the person feels but about giving recognition to their present state. Your choice of words needs to reflect how you connect emotionally to the situation from both having experienced it first hand and having a strong emotional connection to the other person, in this case, your teen. Together, you will be able to express to your teen your emotional understanding of their broken heart.

Another instance in which you would choose an emotional empathic response would be when a co-worker is grieving the death of an animal companion. You can relate to the pain that comes from losing a pet you've cared for and loved. You know how difficult it can be to try and concentrate on work when you're feeling sad.

In this situation, you could respond to your co-worker by telling them, 'I feel your pain. Losing an animal you loved so dearly is hard.' You are able to let your co-worker know that you understand on an emotional level the hurt they are experiencing in their time of grief. Your response expresses to them an understanding that goes beyond the cognitive realm and into the heart.

Speak with Compassionate Empathy

Your level of commitment to helping the other person can be expressed with compassionate empathic responses. Oftentimes, the people you encounter in life are unable to express their need for help for any number of reasons. Whether it be fear of retribution and shame or a lack of knowing the resources available, you will find few people confident enough to ask for compassion.

You can be a shining light of hope by embracing the skills of compassionate empathic response and recognize when others need you. Asking them 'How can I reduce your worry,' or 'What can I do to help,' paired with a genuine desire to follow through with action can make a world of difference in the other person's life. Your one moment of self-sacrifice for the sake of someone else's well-being can have a greater impact when it's from the heart.

You would use a compassionate empathic response if a friend came to you after losing everything in a house fire. Cognitively, you understand the magnitude of such a tragic event, even without experiencing such a loss personally. In addition, your close relationship with this person gives you a clearer picture of their emotional state and pulls harder on your heartstrings.

In this situation, your choice of words must convey how you understand both what the person may be thinking and how they feel. But most importantly, your compassionate empathic response needs to make clear your desire to take an active role in helping your friend. You may say something like, 'I can't imagine how hard it would be to lose everything. You're a great friend and I am here for you. What can I do to help?'

Your response focuses on both the knowledge aspect and the feelings related to the tragedy. You also are clear to indicate how important they are to you and a willingness to help in any way possible. You must avoid feeling sorry for your friend or discounting their experience with comments such as, 'it's only material things' or 'you should just be thankful to be alive.'

You don't have to search too long before you'll encounter someone facing a tough situation in need of compassion and understanding. Compassionate empathic response requires that you possess a strong desire to help those in need and a desire for making a difference in people's lives. It's a selfless act of humanitarianism that can make a huge impact on a person in their time of struggle.

You will discover that no perfect script exists for any of the three types of empathic response. Finding the right words to convey your message of empathy will become easier the more you practice. You will discover that the harder you work at understanding the needs of the people in your life, the easier it will be to communicate with them and meet those needs.

Chapter 4 Recap

★ Speaking with empathy begins with knowing yourself completely and being willing to get to know others fully. It takes both an open mind and a welcoming heart to master the skills of empathic communication.

★ You must avoid the old habits of advice-giving and self-focus that block your ability to hear and understand the other person's needs. Empathy is a tool of interpersonal connection that lets the other person know you care about their experience.

★ In order to learn how to speak with empathy, you must first understand the three types of responses: cognitive, emotional, and compassionate. As you practice your empathic responses in real situations, you will begin to appreciate the role each type plays in relationships and how to continue improving your communication techniques.

★ As you build rapport with the people in your life, you will find it easier to choose the right words because you have made a commitment to understanding the other person. Human connectivity grows stronger when we each pause for a moment to take time for listening and reflection on the other person's message before choosing how to reply.

Speaking with empathy is an endeavor that will require you to have patience and understanding, especially in those situations where you feel lost. Your empathic strength will grow as you strive to learn about who you are in the eyes of yourself and others. Your ability to speak with the highest level of compassionate empathy begins with a willingness to make a difference, no matter how small it may seem.

In the next chapter, you will learn about the importance of using validating responses and how they influence communication. I will teach you why validation is key to empathic communication and when validating someone's feelings is imperative. In addition to examples of validating statements, I will cover the important aspect of identifying personal boundaries and their effects on empathic communication.

Chapter 5 Validating Responses

Learning how to speak with empathy prepares you for being able to give positive validating responses in your conversations. You build a library of vocabulary related to emotions and thoughts as you learn how to talk to the people you engage with. As you become more fluent in your empathic responses, you'll learn more about those people. Your new deeper level of understanding will help you to improve your relationships with validating responses.

Think back to a conversation where you expressed how passionately you felt about a personal situation or event in your life. Maybe you're excitedly telling them about the dream job that finally came to fruition. Or perhaps, you're telling the person about the reckless driver who almost caused an accident on your way home from the store. What kind of response did you get from the other person? Was it what you had expected or did their comment fall flat in comparison to your level of emotional expression?

When you open yourself to the vulnerability of sharing your feelings with another person, you do so with the expectation of getting a supportive response. Unfortunately, you are often met with comments that the other person thinks are helpful but are actually doing just the opposite. The person may have good intentions with their words, but what they are saying invalidates how you feel.

Let's look at the first example above to see the difference between a validating response and an invalidating response. You tell a friend about the new job to obtain confirmation of the joy this new opportunity will bring.

What you don't expect is for a friend or loved one to discount your excitement with invalidating responses like, 'How lucky for you to get paid a ton to do practically nothing all day.'

Such a reply suggests that what you love to do for a living isn't real work and thus your friend has devalued the worth of your skill and your joy. Compare this invalidation to how you would feel if a friend replied to your good news with a validating response. 'Wow! That's fantastic that all your hard work has paid off.' See how different those two situations feel?

You also seek out validation from others when you have negative experiences. You tell your friend about almost getting hit by another car that failed to stop at the four-way intersection while driving home. You're expressing to them your frustrations with how bad the drivers are and how dangerous it's getting just going to the store.

Your friend could respond with, 'You freak out too much over nothing. You didn't get hit so what's the big deal?' Or, they could reply with, "Oh goodness! People like that are so irresponsible.' Which of these two versions of the friend are you most likely to share your feelings with in the future? Without a doubt, you'll choose the empathic and validating friend who offered justification for your feelings about the dangers of bad drivers.

You need the skill of validating responses at work when speaking with co-workers, customers, or clients in your profession. You may need to be supportive when a co-worker shows they are feeling overwhelmed by the amount of work they have to complete. They may say something like, 'I just don't think I can get it all done.'

You can choose to say, 'this new assignment has a crushing amount of paperwork. I can understand feeling stunned by how much you have to do.' This response is empathic toward their feelings of exhaustion and recognizes the reason behind the feeling. Your response normalizes their feeling giving validation to their reality.

And frankly, it is far more positive and uplifting than an invalidating comment such as, 'I guess you'll just have to work harder to keep up.' A judging statement that implies they haven't been working hard already will certainly drag down company morale. Remember that validating responses are a tool to encourage positive thinking and improve self-esteem.

Validating responses at home is a tool to improve communication with your spouse to prevent an argument. You get home from work and realize you forgot to pick up the dry cleaning, again. Your spouse is furious and yells, 'you don't care enough about my career to remember I needed that outfit for my interview tomorrow.' Your validating response of, 'I'm sorry for forgetting again, I can understand your hurt in thinking I don't care. How can I help?'

By first taking responsibility for your mistake instead of making up some excuse, you let them know you did wrong. By empathizing with their feelings, you give them assurance you do indeed care about their feelings. Your offer of wanting to make amends by asking how you can fix it, ensures you want to show support for their career.

What is Validation?

In its basic form, validation addresses two things about the message being communicated. First, your validating response focuses on properly identifying the specific emotion the other person is feeling and expressing in their communication. The second aspect of your response offers justification to the other person that their emotional response to the situation was warranted.

When you give validation to someone's emotional expression, you are providing them a clear and direct message that confirms their situation is real. It tells the other person you see their experience is founded in logic and an understandable outcome of their circumstances. Your validation creates a mutual level of understanding that reduces the risk of conflict in your relationship, leading to a harmonious resolution.

On the other hand, someone who is emotionally incompetent will perceive your expressed emotion as a personal attack and become defensive to your message. Rather than validating your feelings and being open to discuss the issue, they pitch blame at you for the problem. You'll be met with an unwillingness to take on any responsibility and in time, stop trying. Developing healthy interpersonal relationships balances upon how much freedom you have to express your thoughts and feelings about the world around you.

Before you can engage in the confirmation of someone else's feelings, you must have a healthy sense of your own self-validation. Having self-confidence and emotional security comes from positive self-talk. Trusting in yourself by being aware of your strengths and willing to improve your weaknesses gives you greater insight to help others.

Validation is a communication tool that reduces your level of emotional pain and perceived suffering by normalizing the experience. Your pain and suffering feel more extreme when you believe that you are alone in your misery and distress. Feelings of isolation and aloneness intensify your experience of anguish, which in turn, increases your emotional discomfort. Validation shows you that other people understand your circumstances.

It provides a sense of relief and promotes an opportunity to build feelings of security. It's a spark of positivity and a glimmer of hope that can change the path you're taking. Giving validation to someone's experience ultimately restores balance to their self-worth.

Emotional validation is also a key component to the healthy development of children into adulthood. By validating the child's expressed emotion, you begin to guide them on the journey of regulating their emotions. It teaches them the importance of understanding what is going on internally, both in heart and mind, and associating those thoughts and feelings with their actions.

Validation helps them to build a strong connection of self-awareness and a solid foundation of self-esteem. You have the power to set them off in the right direction by encouraging their expression of feelings and maintaining emotional competence. Using validation helps them to learn how to recognize emotional expressions and how they affect others. This is what you see happening when one kid is crying and the others cry in response to the first child's expression of pain.

Steps to Provide Emotional Validation

The first step you must take to provide emotional validation is being fully present and actively listening to the other person. You must possess complete mindfulness of the conversation and the message being expressed. Proper identification of the expressed emotion relies on paying full attention to the messenger's actions and words.

You may find that you'll need to get additional information to help you accurately identify how the person is feeling or what they are thinking. Ask questions that seek to confirm what you understand with regard to the emotion. You can't give someone validation if you've misunderstood how they are feeling.

After someone has shared their emotions with you, pause for a moment to evaluate all of the components of their message. Take time to fully digest their experience to help you process the sequence of events and the emotional outcome. Choose appropriate empathic dialogue that lets them know you understand what they're feeling and why.

In most instances of validation, you don't need to share your own story of a similar experience to show how well you understand their situation. Interjections of this nature can detract from the person's needs when the focus shifts to yourself. However, you may encounter situations of intense emotion that would warrant sharing your own comparable trauma.

Validation's focus is on their experience so keep any personal sharing brief to make the connection quickly. Be mindful not to confuse your emotions from your experience with the emotions they are feeling from their trauma. Your purpose for connecting on this level is to reassure the other person of your relatability to their experience. This will encourage some people to want to share more. Be available to continue listening when those individuals choose to open up to you. Maintain trust in the relationship by having respectful and honest conversations. Follow through when you commit to offering your help in meeting their needs.

Take ownership of any role you played in causing their pain or suffering. Your interactions with others are a collaboration of each person's words and actions. Each of us has the responsibility of self-control in both what we say and how we treat each other. If they tell you something you've said or done has hurt them, recognize their pain.

Confirm with the other person whether or not the discussion has concluded. Have you helped them to meet their emotional needs? Do they feel like their message has been understood and respected? Most importantly, make the changes you need to prevent a repeat of the injury. Your situations stay the same when you keep walking the same old path.

Avoid Committing Invalidation

Your words carry with them both an intended meaning and an interpreted meaning. You may have had good intentions when you said, 'Thank goodness it was only the garage that caught fire.' But your neighbor interprets your words to mean nothing important was lost inside the garage- - the same garage where he was restoring his late father's '76 Corvette.

When you downplay someone's thoughts or feelings you are discounting their experience instead of giving validation to it. You don't see what the big deal is from your perspective of 'it's just a garage' until you learn what value it had to your neighbor. What may seem like an inconvenience to one person could be disastrous for someone else.

Statements of invalidation will either reject, judge, or ignore the other person's feelings. Telling someone, 'you can't be mad about that,' refutes how they are feeling and implies they are wrong to be upset. When you say things like, 'of course you would say something like that,' your invalidating response is both judging their character and attacking them personally.

Ignoring the other person's feelings may be the most hazardous of the three types of invalidation. It keeps the person trapped in their conflict. Without validation, you become confused about how you feel, creating self-doubt. You start to question your own thinking when you find yourself alone in your belief. Validation takes away the uncertainty.

What Validation Doesn't Do

Giving validation to someone's experience does not mean you are rejecting your own reality over theirs. Your friend sees his recent job loss as an exciting opportunity to test the waters of an entirely different career adventure. You can still validate the excitement of his emotional expression while still seeing such a life event as terrifying,

You will encounter any number of situations where the same situation can elicit polar opposite responses from different people. One person may feel apprehensive about moving to a foreign country while another may see it as the greatest thing to ever happen. Validation is an acknowledgment of their experience regardless of how it compares to your perception of the situation.

Validation does not mean you agree with the way the other person thinks or feels. You can give validation to how someone feels while still disagreeing with the circumstances leading to now. Your co-worker tells you how mad they are about their spouse finding out about a gambling debt.

Validation tells your co-worker you get why they might react with anger but that doesn't mean you condone they were keeping a damaging secret. You have an opportunity to connect with the other person using validation that will build trust. Once that bridge of safety is established, they will be more open to the advice and assistance you can offer them.

You are not giving acceptance of their harmful thoughts or behaviors when you respond with validation. You are merely acknowledging the thought or feeling they have expressed with recognition of why they see what they see. Validation doesn't mean you feel sorry for them or their struggle, but rather it means you are able to see their side of the situation.

If a friend confided in you that they felt like a failure after getting fired again, you wouldn't say, 'you're absolutely right to feel like a failure.' Your validation is not an act of agreeance to their emotion so your choice of words needs to show you get how they feel. In this case, you could respond with, 'you feel like success is out of reach.'

When you fail to give validation to the people in your life, you are telling them you're unsupportive and without understanding. You will find that those people will stop opening up to you in their time of need.

Communication will shut down and your relationship will certainly falter and fail when you no longer understand one another.

Barriers to Validation

As you practice using validating responses in your daily life, you may encounter one of two barriers that block your ability to validate. Each one of these obstructions occurs because of your mindset and approach to the situation. Both of these validation barriers can be unlearned once you recognize them and the problems they cause.

The first barrier that can restrict your ability to express validation is called limiting beliefs. A barrier of limiting beliefs means that you have a predetermined limitation set with regard to proper emotional response. Simply put, your beliefs have put restrictions on the way people are expected to react emotionally.

For example, believing that boys shouldn't cry is a limiting belief of emotional expression. It restricts the normal act of crying to only be expressed by girls. You can see why this is problematic in that it wrongfully labels feeling sad as being weak and it devalues those who cry.

Putting these types of limitations on someone's emotional expression could result in that person suppressing their emotions when you're around. Or it could cause the person to overreact in future situations when they have been holding back for so long. If you're in a relationship where you are prohibited from expressing yourself, you're more likely to begin acts of self-harm as a way to cope.

The second barrier that will keep you from giving effective validation is focusing only on positivity. This way of thinking gives the impression that you have to feel a certain way in order to be accepted by others. Feeling anything other than happiness and good fortune means no one wants you around raining on their sunny day.

Trying to overrule their negative feelings with forced positivity generally makes the other person feel worse, not better. If you're always trying to look on the bright side of everything, you'll fail to see the problem in need of being repaired. You can't ignore their negative experience and jump ahead to cheering them up without first letting them grieve.

Validating Personal Boundaries

The quality of your interpersonal relationships is guided by the health of your personal boundaries. If you have healthy personal boundaries, your relationships will flourish. When you have unhealthy boundaries or undefined limitations in your relationships, you may start to feel resentment towards the boundary violator.

Setting personal boundaries isn't about keeping people away. You set these different boundaries to define your individuality. Healthy personal boundaries in your relationships offer a balance of meeting the needs of both people. Validation of personal boundaries creates a harmonious environment in which the relationship can grow and mature.

Establishing healthy personal boundaries begins with being able to identify your needs and desires in each of the five boundary types. It will require you to have the confidence to vocalize those identified boundaries without fear of setting limits. How can you expect others to meet your expectations if you haven't clued them in on what you're expecting?

Types of Personal Boundaries

Once you've gained a better understanding of the different types of personal boundaries, you will become more comfortable with expressing your needs. Self-awareness is often the essential key you need to unlock the mystery of what's deficient in your life. The same knowledge will enhance your ability to validate the personal boundaries of others as you start to understand what they need from you.

Physical Boundaries

The most familiar type of personal boundary that comes to mind for most people is your physical boundaries. Commonly known as your personal space, this boundary defines how comfortable you are with being physically contacted by others. Do you prefer a simple handshake when greeting a friend or do you go for the full bear hug?

Physical boundaries also pertain to your needs associated with basic survival. Your levels of hunger, thirst, and energy are all components of your physical needs and limitations. Communicating to others that you're grabbing some lunch first lets them know that your physical boundary of hunger needs to be met before you can continue.

You can express your physical boundaries with statements such as, 'I didn't get much sleep last night so I need a quick nap before we go out.' You have given a clear indication of what you need, rest, and how it impacts the relationship—which is being able to go out later. When you are able to freely express your physical boundaries in a relationship, people will begin to feel comfortable doing the same.

Violations of your physical boundaries can include unwanted or inappropriate touching such as a shoulder massage or placing their hand on your body. Other types of physical boundary violations that occur involve the denial of basic needs. Making someone continue to work when they are exhausted is a transgression against their physical boundary.

Emotional Boundaries

Your emotional boundaries pertain to the amount of emotional energy you give out and how much you can take in from others. This type of personal boundary incorporates your comfort level with what emotions you express to the people you encounter. It also takes into account what level of emotional conversation you feel comfortable hearing from others.

Creating your emotional boundaries requires you to be able to respect how other people feel and in what way they choose to express those feelings. Healthy emotional boundaries help you develop a sense of when to share and when not to share. It guides your regulation of what you communicate. Unhealthy boundaries or lack of respect for emotional boundaries will teach you to limit what you share and with whom.

You express emotional boundaries when you tell a loved one 'I'm really anxious about your trip. Can we talk about the route you're taking?' You're telling the person both what you are feeling (anxiety) and the need (knowing the route) that they can meet to resolve the emotional conflict. A validating response to this scenario might sound like, 'I understand your worry. Let's go over the itinerary.'

Someone has violated your emotional boundaries if they criticize how you are feeling or try to dismiss what you are experiencing. Trying to make you give justification for how you feel or telling you what you should be feeling only add to the problem. Another form of emotional boundary violation occurs when you invade someone's personal information like their text messages or diary.

Time Boundaries
Another familiar type of personal boundary you experience in daily life is time boundaries. You establish work schedules or school schedules, sports schedules, and even travel schedules to manage your time. Setting time boundaries defines your priorities where precedence is often determined by the level of importance.

You prioritize how you spend your time to ensure that you fulfill all of your obligations. You take time to eat when you're hungry and schedule appointments to take time for self-care. Establishing healthy time boundaries keeps you from overextending yourself or double booking your availability. Setting limits to how much time you spend on things will reduce the risk of sacrificing one for another.

Your ability to create healthy time boundaries means you're able to tell a friend, 'I have to work that weekend,' and they'll understand. It also means having respect for other people's time boundaries. Asking a co-worker if they have a moment to talk instead of just barging into their office to vent about the meeting shows respect for the co-worker's time boundary.

Violations of your time boundaries happen when someone wants you to work for free or they keep you beyond the agreed-upon time. You disrespect someone's time boundaries when you show up late to an interview or when you have to cancel plans because you forgot about your nephew's graduation party.

Intellectual Boundaries
Your thoughts, ideas, and curiosities begin to develop the moment you start to experience life. Setting limits to your intellectual boundaries means not letting others belittle your way of thinking. Having a healthy intellectual boundary is being able to respect an idea that differs from yours without feeling threatened.

Intellectual boundaries are often the source of your agreeing to disagree conflicts with the people in your life. You each have a solidly built belief based on your personal experience and due to the polar opposite outcomes, you have differing opinions of the same situation. Giving validation to one another's intellectual boundary means you're willing to understand their different line of thought.

While everyone is entitled to have an opinion, it does not give you the right to violate someone's intellectual boundary with offensive or hate-filled thinking. You have a right to set limits with regard to ideas or thoughts that are inherently dangerous. You are allowed to tell someone, 'I am not ok with this conversation,' when it is in violation of your intellectual boundary.

Material Boundaries

Your personal possessions such as your car, your home, and everything in your house are extensions of you. Creating material boundaries means you have set limits on what of yours can be borrowed, who may borrow it, and for how long. It can also include parameters with regard to what condition you expect the item to be returned in.

Material boundaries establish your clear expectations of how your things are to be treated when it is in someone else's hands. You may have set limits to how far your teen can travel when driving your car. Or that it must be returned with a full tank of gas and clear of any messes inside and out. Having respect for other people's property is a sign you have healthy material boundaries.

Violations of your material boundaries can include a roommate borrowing your clothes and keeping them for longer than they agreed upon. Perhaps you have a co-worker who is always using your coffee creamer without asking or offering to 'get the next one.' Maybe you have a relative who only calls when they need to 'borrow a few bucks until they get paid next week.'

Creating healthy material boundaries will help you to recognize when someone tries to use money and possessions to control the relationship. You will have the knowledge to see the difference between compassionate generosity and manipulative compensation. When you express your material boundaries, you let others know where you draw the line with your assets and estate.

When to Validate and Why

A psychologist by the name of John Gottman uncovered the secret about your interactions that accurately predicts the success of your relationships. He discovered that how your partner chooses to respond to your emotional expression foretells the success or failure of the relationship. He studied how newlyweds interacted with one another during a weekend stay at a bed and breakfast where he noticed the pattern.

Dr. Gottman found that the success of your relationships with people all hinges on which way they chose to validate your attempt at connecting. He noticed that you have three different options to choose from when giving validation. You can respond with positive validation that shows you are interested in their emotional connection. Or you can respond with either a negative rejection of their feelings or passive appeasement with faked enthusiasm.

For example, your partner says, 'Wow, look at this kitchen' as you tour an open house. They have shared with you their admiration and your reaction will indicate if your feelings connect. You have the option to give positive validation by saying, 'there's so much room and natural light, just like you've wanted.' Your response confirms you agree with their excitement and joy of the room and it also gives cues to how well you know your partners need for a spacious, well-lit kitchen.

A passive validation to your partner's love for the kitchen would sound like, 'yeah, it's nice.' You don't disagree with their emotional expression but your lack of enthusiasm is apparent. If however, you chose to respond in a negative manner that rejects their feelings you might say, 'ugh, these colors are hideous! Who paints a kitchen like this?' Your response ignores their expression of joy and stomps all over it with your personal disgust for something they just expressed liking.

Throughout your day-to-day life, you make requests for emotional connection with the people you encounter. You tell a story to a co-worker about how exhilarated you were after a fishing trip over the weekend. You vent to a friend about the traffic jam that made you late for an important meeting. You're in search of that feeling you get when the other person feels your victory or defeat.

Dr. Gottman's study determined that the couples who were still together at the 6-year mark gave positive validation to their partner 90% of the time. For those couples who split up during the 6 year follow-up period, positive validation had only been used 33% of the time. Your relationship success depends almost entirely on meeting each other's emotional needs through genuine validation.

Healthy and positive validation is important to your relationships for a number of reasons. Your positive validation expresses to them your acceptance of who they are. It shows them that you value their beliefs and feelings. It tells them you understand the needs they have and the boundaries of those desires. Positive validation strengthens your relationships by helping you to regulate your responses to the emotional connections people are trying to make

You develop problems of insecurity and a negative sense of self if your attempts of emotional connection are always met with resentment and hostility. You begin to experience self-doubt when you're frequently told how to feel or that you're wrong to feel as you do. Continued denial of positive validation in your relationships can progress to issues such as anxiety and depression.

Levels of Validation

Once you start to understand what validation does for your relationships, you will begin to recognize what level of validation a situation calls for. The level you give is derived from several factors including how well you know each other and the intensity of the emotional experience being shared. The highest level of validation your relationship can reach increases in relation to your level of knowledge about one another.

Not every relationship or situation will require you to achieve the highest level of validation and some will make use of multiple levels at the same time. You will find times where the first level of validation is sufficient to meet the person's need and others that will require your all. While it may seem very confusing at first, you will begin to make sense of it after you learn the six levels of validation.

Level 1 - Being Present and Mindful

You are engaged in first-level validation when you hold someone's hand in a comforting gesture during a physically painful event. Level one validation is what you do as you're listening to your child describe their first day of soccer practice. Present and mindful validation means driving to your best friend's house to be with them after their spouse's funeral so they don't have to mourn alone.

Level one validation is being there physically and emotionally for someone. You use this level of validation in any number of day-to-day life events. Something as simple as holding the elevator for a co-worker who is stuck with an armload of boxes is an expression of level one validation. You were mindful of their hands being too full to hit the call button and you physically took action to help.

As you can see from the examples, the amount of effort you put forth can vary based on factors such as the closeness of the relationship, the action being required, and the physical boundaries of each person. For instance, you are more likely to offer a hug to friends and family when greeting them at a birthday party versus the handshake you give when greeting a neighbor at a kid's birthday.

Level 2 - Accurate Reflection

Validation at this level means you are able to accurately summarize the thought or emotion in need of being recognized and accepted. You may be in a situation that requires you to correctly reflect back on your understanding of what validation the other person needs from you. Or you may find yourself reflecting internally about what it is you are lacking from others.

You use accurate reflection when helping someone to verbalize the emotions they are experiencing. In this level of validation, you can help them to work through the situation. Accurate reflection gives you the tools to separate rationale from the emotion so each can be examined. By addressing each aspect, you can validate their experience and still hold a different viewpoint.

A friend calls you in a fit of anger. His bank recently denied him a second mortgage based on his current household income. You can use level two validation to express your understanding of being upset about having his hopes shattered for an upgrade to his family's home. You can also maintain an understanding from the bank's point of view because he may not be able to make the new payments.

Level 3 - Guessing the Emotion

The third level of validation is reached when you are able to guess what the person is thinking or feeling when they haven't expressed it directly. You know them well enough that you are able to decipher clues from both what they have said and the nonverbal cues. You are able to distinguish the difference between excitement and anxiety.

You are able to unmask their feelings that they keep hidden by recognizing the patterns of human behaviors. Level three validation can help you coax emotional expressions from those who have been forced to hide how they truly feel or think. It provides you the opportunity to accurately label the feelings being felt and the healthy way in which to express them.

This level of validation requires you to pay close attention to the communication details you get beyond their words. Look for the clues that will help you guess how they feel about what they've shared. You could say, 'I imagine you must be feeling betrayed by her lying,' when a co-worker tells you about their daughter skipping school.

Level 4 - Understand from History

The way you react intellectually and emotionally to different situations is based on your life experiences. You develop certain patterns of thinking and feeling based on what has happened to you. The same can be said for everyone else you encounter in your life. For each person, their unique experience shapes their personality, behavior patterns, and emotional expression.

Your knowledge of the other person's past behaviors and experiences gives you a better perspective to understanding their reaction to their current situation. For example, your parent is apprehensive about grocery shopping alone after hearing about someone being mugged at their local store. A validating response in this situation may require you to accompany them on their shopping trips for a while.

You can also experience level four self-validation to help understand your own feelings and reactions. If you were in a car accident, you are likely to be more anxious and cautious the next time you're in a vehicle because of the negative experience. You're better able to cope with these feelings and emotionally recover more quickly when you acknowledge the history behind the reaction.

Level 5 - Normalize the Emotion

Validation occurs at this level when you agree that anyone would react in the same way. You are able to relate to the other person's reaction because it's what's to be expected from the circumstances. Discovering that someone dented your brand new car while you were at the bank would make anybody upset.

When you find that the person responded in a logical manner, you are validating the normalcy of their expression. You are able to understand why they feel as they do because everyone would feel that way if it happened to them. You express level-five validation when you tell your friend, 'it's perfectly normal to be nervous about moving to a new place.'

You are giving validation to the commonality of the other person's thoughts and feelings. You are giving them assurance that their reaction is acceptable and a logically anticipated response to their situation. You confirm with them that they are right to think or feel as they do.

Level 6 - Radical Genuineness

The highest level of validation you can give someone is known as radical genuineness. In this state, you are able to connect with people at their deepest emotional level. Typically, you reach this level of validation if you experienced a similar situation being expressed.

You have a comparative life event that gives you a richer understanding of the experience. Being able to see the equivalence of your situation to theirs can provide a clearer picture of what they might need. Reaching the level of radical genuineness means you have a greater appreciation for the human spirit and inner strength needed for survival.

Your thoughts and feelings are what makes you vulnerable to being hurt. Knowledge about why you think and feel what you do gives you the strength to heal. Providing the people in your life the right level of validation for their needs secures a future of healthy relationships.

Types of Validating Responses

You learn how to craft an effective validation response once you understand the different purposes they serve. Giving the right form of validation means you understand both the emotion in need of validation and the type of understanding being sought. Over time, you will become better at being able to know what others need from you and provide the appropriate response.

Acknowledgment

You will discover that many people are just looking for someone to understand them when seeking validation. You take notice of their emotional state. Then you provide a verbal acknowledgment to confirm you see what they mean. A friend tells you they just lost their job. You can see that your friend is on the brink of crying. To acknowledge your friend's feelings, you might say, 'I can see you're really upset by this news,' or 'losing a job can feel overwhelming.'

Your choice of exact words will always depend on the circumstances of the situation. You also have to consider your relationship with the other person and be respectful with the words you choose to speak.

Interest

Often you will find people are gauging your level of interest when they chose to share something with you. You can express how much you care about their situation with validation statements of interest. These statements reflect your desire for wanting to know more about how they are feeling.

Your child comes home from auditions and seems discouraged. Not sure of how things went, you can show interest in their emotional state by asking, 'How do you think it went?,' or 'How are you feeling about your audition?'

It's always ok to check with the person about how they're feeling when you're not certain about the details of the event.

These types of validating statements are extremely helpful to building relationships through shared interests. Your spouse wants you to take a pottery class together because they loved it years ago back in school. By giving validation to their desire to include you in their interest, you're telling them you want to be included. You open yourself to greater life experiences by connecting and sharing your passions with others.

Reaction
You will experience occasions where the person is in search of your reaction to what they've shared with you. Your emotional response to their situation can help them evaluate your level of understanding. You give reactive validation to clarify your own feelings about what the other person has told you.

This type of validating response gives you the opportunity to tell a friend, 'I can't imagine what you must be feeling,' when you don't know. Or you can tell them, 'it hurts to find out you felt all alone that day,' when you do know. Like all communication should be, your reactive validation needs to be honest and express your true feelings and understanding.

You're not always going to know how you feel about something shared with you and that's ok. As long as you tell the truth about what you think and feel, you're doing your part to connect with others. When you're not honest with who you are, you'll never be able to develop effective interpersonal relationships at home, work, or anywhere.

Grateful
Sometimes, you will be in situations where the other person needs to feel appreciated for their input and attentiveness. With this type of validation, your goal is to express your gratitude for their sharing of thoughts and

feelings. You give them confirmation that you value their input about the situation.

You should express validation of being grateful to someone who exhibits the courage to vocalize what they need from your relationship. When a loved one tells you they're concerned about what the doctor said at your last appointment, it's because they care. Your validating response of gratitude means telling them, 'I'm so glad to know how much you care about my well-being.'

At work, you can show the coworker you appreciate their new idea by telling them so. You could say, 'thank you for pointing this out. I hadn't considered that,' when they share the negative impact a change is going to cause and a possible solution they've found. It would do the world a huge favor if everyone took the time to be more grateful for one another.

Supportive
You reach out to connect with other people when you're in need of support. You may be looking for someone to be supportive of a major decision that impacts the relationship. Or you may just need to know who you can count on in an emergency.

Supportive validating responses let the other person know you've got their back. You might say, 'I'll be there to help load the truck,' when a friend breaks the news they're moving. Not only are you providing the physical help they might need, but you are also expressing emotional support in favor of their big change.

The people in your life need to feel confident you approve of who they are in thought and action. You share your dreams and goals with those people who boost you towards success. Showing someone you can offer supportive validation is as easy as asking them, 'What can I do to help?'

Encouraging

Along with being supportive, your validating responses can provide encouragement to the other person. All too often, you hear the discouraging words of what you did wrong. Imagine how great your days would be if you received a wealth of encouragement.

Giving a person validation of encouragement boosts their confidence. You build up their self-image when you give praise to their efforts. Telling your child, 'I'm so proud of how hard you worked,' encourages them to keep being a hard worker. Letting others know you believe in them, helps them to believe in themselves.

Encouraging validation is a great way to let others know how they can meet your needs. When someone's actions positively impact the relationship, you can give encouraging validation such as, 'your strength is unwavering,' to tell them how strong you think they are. In the same sense, you can use this type of validation to encourage making alternate choices to bad decisions such as, 'I trust you to make the right choice.'

Whichever type of validating response you need to use, remember to be truthful in what you say without disrespect for their truth. Your ability to influence the thoughts and feelings of others should never be about control. Validating responses are a tool you can use to facilitate healthy communication in every relationship.

Chapter 5 Recap

★ Validating responses give you a voice to reply to the emotional needs of others. They provide a framework of communication that expands as you build your relationship.

★ Providing others with validation means you recognize their emotional expression and justify their condition. You verbalize to them your commonality of life experiences and communicate your level of understanding.

★ Your relationships rely on active participation in communicating personal needs by both parties. Healthy relationships occur when both individuals know and respect each other's personal boundaries: physical, emotional, time, intellectual, and material.

★ Accurate validation responses require you to know why the person is seeking validation and what level is needed. Every situation is a unique combination of what boundaries are involved, what type of validation is being sought, and what level of response will meet their needs.

★ You will begin to develop a greater connection in your relationships when you master the six types of validating responses: Acknowledgment, interest, reaction, grateful, supportive, and encouraging. In time, you'll weave together the perfect combination of types to be fully responsive to people's needs

Validating responses are your contribution to the connection the other person is trying to make. Your relationships with people require that you understand the role each of you plays in the conversation. You respect their personal boundary needs while clearly expressing your own. Healthy relationships thrive when people respond positively to one another's needs. When you actively take part in other people's sharing, you give validation to the relationship. You've put the thoughts and feelings of someone else ahead of your own to provide the strength they need in their time of feeling weak.

In the final chapter, I will show you the action plan that will get your relationships on the right path. I will review what you have learned in the previous chapters with the five keys to effective listening. With the help of real-world examples, I will illustrate how to execute these steps to reach the highest level of powerful listening.

Chapter 6: The Keys to Effective Listening

Right now, you may be feeling overwhelmed by the information overload of trying to remember all of these methods and expectations. You may have doubts about knowing what to say when you're hit with a real conversation. Perhaps you're a bit worried you'll forget which level of empathy is best or what type of validation is being sought. Just remember, every new skill requires frequent practice before it feels natural.

In each chapter, you learned about the individual components that work together when you communicate with others. It was important for you to examine the different aspects of listening at their core in order to be able to recognize the changes you need to make. Learning to recognize how you communicate helps you to identify the ways others communicate too.

In this chapter, I will incorporate all of the key pieces of effective listening into a concise five-step action plan. Each step will begin with a brief description that explains the intent and purpose of that stage. Next, I will outline the important factors associated with each step of effective listening. Finally, I will provide real-world scenarios to demonstrate the five steps in action at home, work, and during social engagements.

Step One: Preparation

Your purpose for actively preparing to listen is to create a calm and quiet environment that welcomes open and honest expression of thoughts and feelings. You make preparations that ensure clear communication can occur uninterrupted. You prepare to listen with the purpose of having a conversation that ends with resolution and some level of positivity.

Your intent for preparing to actively listen is to develop a stronger rapport with the other person through understanding their worldview. You enter into the conversation with the intent of learning more about the people in your life. Your preparations are made with the goal of reaching a deeper level of connection to those around you.

Clear Away All Distractions

External distractions like televisions and electronic devices need to be turned off or put away. Shutting off potential interruptions keeps both individuals focused on the conversation. Giving your full attention to the other person indicates you are interested in communicating.

Internal distractions are not as easy to turn off as your laptop or smartphone. Your mind is always racing with thoughts and ideas about what you have going on in your own life. Clearing away the internal distractions requires you to maintain control of your wandering mind.

Remember the Importance of Meaning

Preparing to listen effectively includes you knowing how important it is to understand their meaning of the words they use to express themselves. Communication that involves emotional expression can be difficult to interpret correctly. This is because your unique life experience built your worldview as did everyone else's experiences built their view.

Your definition of joy or fear may differ from theirs and thus cause a conflict when trying to understand their emotional expression. One man's tragedy is another man's grand adventure. Effective listening requires you to prepare your mindset with the belief system of the person speaking to you.

You can only decipher their message accurately if you know how they are communicating.

Follow the Body Language Clues

Assessing the body language of the other person is a preparatory step that alerts you to their level of comfort or discomfort. You can quickly determine if they are relaxed by their open posture and welcoming demeanor. Conversely, you can see when someone is distressed from the look on their face or the way they sit in their chair.

Eye contact is your way of telling the speaker you are engaged in what they are saying and that they have your interest. Not being able to keep eye contact indicates you're either not interested in the conversation or you're not being honest. Either situation is problematic to open communication and can be detrimental to the relationship.

Body language is a physical demonstration of how you are feeling emotionally. Your calm and relaxed mind will emit positive energy and a stress-free posture. If, however, your mind is stressed, angry, or depressed, your body language will reveal those feelings visually. Keep in mind that your body language has the ability to influence how others feel.

Step Two: Listen Attentively

Your purpose for attentive listening is to make sure you have correctly understood the meaning of the conversation. You won't get all the details and risk seeing the bigger picture if you're not being fully attentive to the speaker. It is often this very important step, that tends to get most people into communication troubles.

Your intent behind listening attentively is a show of respect for the other person and what they have to say. You have made a conscious decision to make time for someone else's needs with an end goal of positive changes and growth. You listen attentively with the intention of building healthy relationships with the people in your life.

Show Your Attentiveness

Your eye contact tells the speaker your focus is on them and what they are saying to you. In addition, your mind is better able to accurately process the situation and the meaning of the message when you are looking at the person speaking.

Your facial expressions react to the emotions you feel and can be great indicators of your level of actively listening. Smiling in agreeance or in reaction to a positive statement shows them you're listening. You can also signal to the speaker you don't understand with a facial expression of confusion.

Your body's posture shows your level of interest and attentiveness. You can sit in a way that tells the other person you're paying attention by facing the speaker. Your body positioning can also tell the speaker you're ready to exit the conversation by leaning away.

Verbalize Your Attentiveness

You can use any of the six verbal indicators of active listening alone or in combination to show you are attentive to the conversations.

❖ Positive reinforcement is the use of responses like, 'I see' or 'indeed' to affirm you are in agreeance or understanding. Used sparingly, it can encourage the speaker to continue; use too much and it becomes condescending.

❖ Remembering key aspects of their message when giving responses tells the speaker you paid attention to the details. It also builds confidence in the person when you are able to recall something significant to them.

❖ Questions can be a way for you to get the speaker to elaborate on their thoughts or feelings to get more details about the story. This gives you an opportunity to obtain more information to help you identify their thoughts and feelings correctly.

❖ Clarification questions are used when you are not 100% clear about what the other person is thinking or feeling. These questions help you clear up any miscommunications or misunderstandings you have during the conversation.

❖ Reflection, like a mirror, helps you get a better view of the conversation by checking with the speaker to see that you've gotten the picture. You can reflect either thoughts or feelings to help decipher the message accurately.

❖ Summarization of both the thought and feelings tells the speaker you were fully attentive to their words and emotional expression. You tell the speaker you understand their message completely when you can retell their experience.

Choose a Communication Style

You have four different styles of communication to choose from when using verbal indicators for active listening.

❖ Paraphrasing is a method of restating the speaker's message for context in your own words without changing the meaning or adding your own interpretations.

❖ Reflecting feelings helps you to pinpoint the speaker's mood and emotional expression of their experience.

- ❖ Reflecting meaning helps you to remove the emotional component and focus your understanding on the thoughts and actions of the person's experience.
- ❖ Summaritive reflection combines the aspects of reflecting feelings and reflecting meaning to understand the person's experience in its entirety.

Avoid Active Listening Blockers

- ❖ Don't try to read their mind in an attempt to predict the path of the conversation. Listen to what they are saying and follow their lead.
- ❖ Don't rehearse in your mind what you plan to say in response to their message. You may miss their point and end up being off the mark with your reply.
- ❖ Don't filter what you're hearing by only choosing to listen to what pleases you. You have to be open to listening to a truth that may be painful to face.
- ❖ Don't come to the conversation with preconceived judgments about the person or their ideas and abilities. Active listening means you are accepting of differing opinions and perceptions of the situation.
- ❖ Don't space off or begin daydreaming about a personal memory that the conversation may have sparked. This is about their experience and needs and your focus should reflect so.
- ❖ Don't start spouting out advice on how they should think or feel about their situation. Active listening is about understanding them, not changing their mind.
- ❖ Don't begin a sparring match with the other person by being oppositional and turning their situation into an argument.
- ❖ Don't expect to always be right about situations in your relationships. This is an aggressive stance that prevents you from finding common ground.

❖ Don't derail the conversation in order to avoid discussing the presenting problem. This is a destructive tactic that only creates more conflict.

❖ Don't placate the other person by blindly agreeing with everything they think and feel. This will prevent you from helping them to see the solution to their situation.

❖ Don't try to compare yourself to everyone you converse with to feel good about yourself. We all have inherent value we gain from our unique experiences and shouldn't base self-worth on the better or worse lives of others.

❖ Don't feel like you have to share a comparative story to try and identify with the other person's experience. This detracts from their situation and puts the focus on you instead.

❖ Don't dismiss the other person's thoughts or feelings as this tells them you see them as inferior or that you are rejecting their reality.

Active Listening Enhancers

❖ Strong eye contact helps you to maintain your focus on the speaker. You are much more attentive to what is being said when your eyes are on who is speaking.

❖ Resist the urge to jump in with your own thoughts before they have finished speaking. Wait patiently until they have finished before you offer any reply.

❖ Keep an open mind about the situation and be willing to work together on a solution.

❖ Get a complete picture of the situation and ask questions to ensure you are understanding the other person correctly.

❖ Provide them with a commitment to reach the agreed-upon goal to resolve their conflict.

Step Three: Reflect Empathetically

Your purpose for reflecting empathetically is to express how well you understand the worldview of their experience. Your empathic expressions let them know you see the situation as they do. You tell them through empathy that you get why they feel as they do.

Your intentions for using reflective empathy are to make a deeper connection with the other person intellectually and emotionally. Your goal is to build a stronger relationship by actively feeling their joys and sorrows with them. Reflecting empathetically requires your intentions to be positive influences on the conversation.

Types of Empathy

❖ Cognitive empathy refers to your empathizing with the way the other person is thinking. Their logic is backed by the facts of the experience. You're able to relate to their thinking because their mindset is rational.

❖ Affective empathy is your ability to share the same emotional interpretation of the experience and understand why. You are able to connect by understanding how they feel.

❖ Somatic refers to the type of empathy where you physically experience the other person's emotional expression.

Avoid Empathy Barriers

❖ Your way of thinking can result in cognitive bias. You must look beyond your mindset of right versus wrong in order to be able to see where the other person is coming from.

❖ Your empathy can be blocked by dehumanizing the other person's experience. Don't assess someone's level of suffering based on your perception of their hardships.

❖ Empathy's final barrier occurs when you place blame on the person for their present circumstances. This prevents you from recognizing factors of the situation that are the real influencers of the conflict.

Stages of Empathy

You will progress through the stages of empathy with each new relationship you develop in your personal and professional life.

❖ Stage 1 - Use their exact wording when making empathic statements and responses
❖ Stage 2 - Paraphrase their message by using your own vocabulary choices of similar meaning
❖ Stage 3 – Reflect their feelings being expressed
❖ Stage 4 – Reflect both the feeling and meaning of their message

Speak with Empathy

Cognitive empathic responses are used so that your focus is on the logic and facts of the person's experience. Emotional empathic responses keep your focus on addressing the emotional aspect of the person's conflict. Compassionate responses incorporate the person's cognitive perceptions and emotional expressions with your desire to help alleviate their suffering.

Step Four: Offer Validation

The purpose of offering your validation is to confirm to the speaker that their experience was real. You give them a sense of feeling normal when you validate their thoughts or feelings.

Your intention for validating their situation is not about assessing right versus wrong. Rather, it is a justification of how they feel or believe based on the circumstances of their experience.

Identify the Personal Boundary

Conflict arises from crossing someone's boundary. In order to give accurate validation to the problem, you must first identify the boundary that's been violated. This includes the following:

- Physical -personal space
- Emotional - feelings
- Time - allotment of focus
- Intellect - way of thinking
- Material - personal possessions and finances

Determine Required Level of Validation

Review the following levels and determine which is most suitable for the situation:

Level 1 - Being present and mindful of their needed validation
Level 2 - Accurate reflection of how they perceive the situation
Level 3 - Guessing the emotion they're not verbalizing
Level 4 - Understanding their situation from their history of experiences
Level 5 - Normalizing their feeling to assure anyone would feel the same
Level 6 - Radical Genuineness is the deepest level of emotional connection you can reach with another

Types of Validation

Choose one or more of the six types of validating responses.

- ❖ Acknowledgment of their situation lets them know you noticed their emotional expression and understand their feelings and thoughts.
- ❖ Show them you are interested in what they have shared with you to let them know you care about the things they care about.
- ❖ React with the emotions or thoughts you are feeling as they pertain to the experience or conflict they have shared with you.
- ❖ Be grateful for the open and honest communication of their thoughts or feelings and people will feel more comfortable sharing more.
- ❖ Be supportive of their experience to let them know they can count on you to share in their joy or hold them up when they're down.
- ❖ Show encouragement for their positive thoughts and actions to build their self-esteem and forge a stronger relationship.

Step Five: Confirm Completion

Your purpose for confirming that the conversation has concluded is to verify with the speaker that their message has been received. You allow the speaker to determine if their message has been heard clearly and accurately. Your goal in getting confirmation of completion is to let the other person know you are interested in their satisfaction of resolve.

Your intent should not be about being the decision-maker regarding your level of understanding. You are to confirm whether they feel you understand them. This can be different from what you feel you understand. This is what makes confirmation of collaborative resolve important.

This final step is often the one that people fail to achieve. You believe that the problem has been resolved because the other person has stopped speaking. But, sometimes the reason they've gone quiet is out of defeat. You must ask them directly if they believe the problem has been resolved or what steps need to be taken next.

When someone needs to be heard, you must not only actively listen. You must take all actions required of you to make a difference. You only build half a bridge when you understand the message but do nothing with the material.

You empower the people in your life when you ask them if their need has been met. Let them know you want to hear them and they will continue to speak. Offer all that you can give them in their time of struggle and they will remember you in your time of need.

The next section will provide you with different sceanrios illustrating the 5 steps put to use. We will discuss scenarios at home, at work and with friends.

5-Step Action Plan at Home

Scenario 1

Your spouse is upset about the money you spent from the budget without their knowledge. As a result, the account didn't have enough to cover the grocery purchase. Your spouse had to pick through and put things back to bring the amount down to the available balance.

Step 1: Prepare
You and your spouse start by finding a quiet place to sit down and talk about what happened. You clear your mind of any unrelated issues and keep

your focus on the spouse's experience at the store. Make note of your spouse's body language and word choice to establish their thoughts and feelings about what transpired.

Step 2: Listen Attentively

Allow your spouse to fully express how they are feeling about what happened when they learned the account didn't have enough money. Perhaps they are not so upset by your actions as they were embarrassed in front of strangers for appearing too poor to afford food. Remembering the fact that your spouse has anxieties about such incidents happening helps you to understand the anger.

Step 3: Reflect Empathetically

In this scenario, you could say, 'I understand why you're upset. I know how stressful shopping is for you.' You let your spouse know that how they are feeling is a logical response to the circumstances. You reflect both their mood of anger and the meaning behind the emotion-- stress from social anxiety.

Step 4: Offer Validation

You identify two personal boundaries involved in this situation, emotional (anxiety caused by social embarrassment) and material (spending budget money). Level 5 validation could be used here since most anyone would be upset to find their bank account didn't cover the tab. You can address both broken boundaries with a statement such as, 'You're right to be upset. It was irresponsible of me to spend money without telling you about it. I know how this kind of surprise affects you.'

Step 5: Confirm Completion

Your final step is to ask your spouse if there is anything else that they want to talk about regarding this incident. You can offer to always communicate any money spent immediately so as not to forget in the future. Or this may be a conversation that leads to more talks about how money is handled in the relationship.

Scenario 2

Your spouse asked you to be home from your outing by a certain time so they could make it to an appointment. You and your friends tend to go on and on when telling stories over a few drinks. Now, you've arrived home an hour late to an angry spouse yelling about whether or not you know how to tell time.

Step 1: Prepare

Clear your mind of any excuses you have in your back pocket to explain away why you're being late isn't your fault. They will only make things worse. Find a way to calm the energy in the room with deep breathing and speak in a soothing voice as you sit down to talk.

Step 2: Listen Attentively

Sit facing one another as you listen to your spouse express how it makes them feel when you fail to be home on time. Look into their eyes as they tell you being late tells them what they have to do isn't seen as important to you. You may even choose to get clarification by asking, 'are you saying my being late feels like my time is more important than yours?'

Step 3: Reflect Empathetically

After they have clarified how they are feeling you can express your cognitive understanding, emotional empathy, or both. It's logical for someone to be upset when you're late. You can also relate to how disrespectful it feels to make someone wait beyond a set time frame. You could say something like, 'you feel disrespected by my being late when I knew you had an appointment.'

Step 4: Offer Validation

You encroached upon your spouse's time boundary when you failed to be home when expected. This situation calls for either level 4 or level 5 validation. You can either express understanding from their history intolerance for tardiness or normalize their feelings because many people feel disrespected by someone showing up late.

Step 5: Confirm Completion

You may feel like the apologizing has made amends but that may not be the end of what they have to say. When you are the listener, you must check with the speaker to see that they feel their message has been received. Ask if there is more that you can do to repair the damage done to the relationship.

Scenario 3

Your teen comes home after borrowing the car to go out with friends. When you ask about how their night was, they proceed to tell you about a minor accident involving a mailbox. They explain how an animal darted out after dropping off their friend and swerving to miss it, hitting the mailbox.

Step 1: Preparation

Your first step when preparing to have a conversation with your child is to clear your mind of judgments you may have about what happened. Shut off any external distractions that could prevent you from focusing on the conversation. Keep an open-mind about what they have to say and remember that your job as a parent is to guide them towards making intelligent decisions.

Step 2: Listen Attentively

Eye contact with your child is the best lie detector when you know what to look for. If they are unable to hold your gaze as they tell their story, you'll know to ask more questions. You will see from their body language and hear in the speech whether their words are genuine.

Step 3: Reflect Empathetically
You could express your understanding of the situation using cognitive or affective empathy. You might say, 'I know how much you care about animals and understand why you would swerve to miss hitting one.' Or you could focus more on their emotional response to their situation with, 'you must have been concerned it was someone's pet to risk damaging the car or getting injured yourself.'

Step 4: Offer validation
You can use this opportunity to discuss the material boundaries they have tarnished by damaging both your car and the person's mailbox. Normalizing their feelings is probably the best highest level of validation needed. This is the ideal situation for a parent to use grateful validation by saying, 'thank you for being honest about what happened to the car.'

Step 5: Confirm Completion
You are able to confirm the conversation has reached its goal when a plan of action is established. You and your teen work together to create a plan to address both the damage to the car and the replacement of the broken mailbox. You reach completion when both parties feel the problem has been fully resolved.

Scenario 4
You receive notification from your child's school that indicates they are failing one of their classes. Your child has always done well in school. You also learn they have been skipping the class in question.

Step 1: Preparation
Set aside a time where you and your child can talk about what is going on without interruptions. Turn off all electronic devices that would prevent

either of you from focusing on the conversation. Do not come to the table with preconceived opinions as to why your child is failing.

Step 2: Listen Attentively
Show you care about what is causing them to skip class and fail with open body language that welcomes them to share. Ask questions about the class that will help them to elaborate on the problem. Find out as much detail by checking with them using reflective statements like, 'you're struggling because the teacher doesn't explain the answer.'

Step 3: Reflect Empathetically
Pay close attention to what your child tells you about their experience in the classroom to understand how they feel. Listen for clues that will identify the source of the problem. You may discover it's not the subject matter that your child struggles with but a conflict with the instructor. Let your child know you hear them with, 'I understand that you believe the teacher treats you differently than others in the class.'

Step 4: Offer Validation
Your child's intellectual boundary has been violated by an authority figure. You need to use the highest levels of validation, either normalizing their feelings or radical genuineness. In this particular situation, you might say, 'anyone would skip class to avoid such mistreatment (level5).' Or a level 6 response might look like, 'I know how important school is to you and together, we will get to the bottom of this situation.'

Step 5: Confirm Completion
Your child needs to know first and foremost that you believe them about their experience. This is not a situation where you just tell them to ignore the bully. You will only be able to bring this conversation to a conclusion by actively addressing the source of the problem, the teacher's inappropriate behavior.

5-Step Action Plan at Work

Scenario 1

Your boss has informed you it's time for your annual performance review. It's been a challenging year but you believe you've done your best. Your confidence is not as high, however, because you don't feel like you and your boss are on the same page.

Step 1: Preparation

You need to go in with an open-mind and think as a boss does. Understand that performance reviews are not a personal attack on you but corrective critique of your output. Jobs have purpose, are you fulfilling the purpose according to the company expectation?

Step 2: Listen Attentively

Pay attention with eye contact and actively hear what your boss is telling you. Listen for key points of improvement and reflect back to show you understand. If your boss mentions your lack of responding to company emails is disrupting production, you could say, 'I understand that you're saying prompt responses to emails are important to the process.'

Step 3: Reflect Empathetically

You could express how well you understand your boss's disappointment in your work by using Stage 3 empathy. Your boss will appreciate knowing you are in agreement with their feelings. You could say, 'I understand how you feel disappointed. I agree that communication is important in order for the team to complete their task.'

Step 4: Offer Validation

In this scenario, you have to address the boundaries of the boss's time and material, in this case your paycheck. Your performance output failed to meet the standards of the employment agreement. Using Level 4 validation, your confirmation of this could be stated as, 'Your business is a success because of your strategies and emphasis on communication,' an acknowledgement of their concern.

Step 5: Confirm Completion

Your boss has certain expectations from you and by actively listening to those needs you can improve your work relationship. Be sure to ask any and all clarification questions to determine what you need to do better. Follow-up with your boss to show where you have made improvements to indicate that you care about the success of the business.

Scenario 2

Your employee tells you they are being harassed by a coworker. They explain how they feel embarrassed by the coworker's crude jokes. You listen as they explain how disruptive this person's behavior is to the work day.

Step 1: Preparation

You need to ensure confidentiality is kept in this type of conversation. By talking privately in a secure location, you can provide a safe environment for honest communication. It also will prevent distractions or interruptions from interfering with the conversation.

Step 2: Listen Attentively

You may need to coax more details out of an employee if they are struggling to explain the situation out of fear or embarrassment. If so you could say, 'can you tell me what a typical encounter with the coworker looks like?' You show that you want to understand their experience and worded as such, it can help spark a memory of a recent incident.

Step 3: Reflect Empathetically

As their boss, your type of empathy will most often be cognitive. Affective empathy can occur with a long time employment relationship. In this case, your empathy can focus on understanding the thinking behind why the conflict needs to be addressed. You could say, 'I completely understand how this hostile environment is having a negative impact on you and the rest of our team.'

Step 4: Offer Validation

Your employee is seeking assurance that what they are experiencing is a problem. They are looking to you for confirmation that their conflict with this coworker is a concern to you as well. You could do this with an expression of gratitude. "Thank you for alerting me to this situation. No one should feel uncomfortable at work due to behaviors of a team member.'

Step 5: Confirm Completion

At this stage of the conversation, you should ask the employee if there are any other issues they want to talk about. Allow them the opportunity to determine when they've concluded sharing. Your closing words should include what steps you will take to address the problem. Follow-up with the employee as time passes to seek updates on the work environment.

Scenario 3

A coworker tells you they're worried about the talks of layoffs around the office. Your coworker expresses being afraid of not being able to find another job if they get cut. You listen as they talk about the stress from not being able to provide for their family.

Step 1: Preparation

Clear your thoughts of any preconceived opinions about the coworker or the potential layoffs. Be able to give all of your attention to your coworker.

You may have to set aside a time outside of work to have a valuable conversation.

Step 2: Listen Attentively

Show you are listening with good eye contact and positive body language. Get a better understanding of their situation by asking questions. You could say, "what is your primary worry regarding a possible layoff?' This clarification can help you see the problem from their point of view.

Step 3: Reflect Empathetically

Chances are you and your coworker are in the same boat of uncertainty. Your type of empathy in this case could be effective. However, if you're not feeling their same emotions you can empathize with their thinking with, 'being able to find a new job right away seems to be your biggest concern.

Step 4: Offer Validation

Your coworker may be seeking encouragement or support from you. Your validation level here could be Level 5, normalizing their experience. You could offer encouragement by highlighting their strengths. You might tell them, 'it's normal to be worried about losing your job. Your talent and hard work will always be an asset, wherever you go.'

Step 5: Confirm Completion

Check with your coworker to make sure they've shared what they needed to say. Determine what more you are able to do to help such as talking again in the near future. Let them know to what level you can be of service and support.

5-Step Action Plan with Friends

Scenario 1
Your friend needs to talk to you because they are struggling with an addiction. You listen as they describe their feelings of helplessness. They express to you how scared they are of losing everything; their job, home, and relationships.

Step 1: Preparation
This conversation requires you to let go of any opinions you have about addiction. You have to step into your friend's realm and see their reality. Your focus needs to be lazer sharp and your body language should convey open communication and care.

Step 2: Listen Attentively
Pay close attention to the details of their story to help you remember the specific struggle they are having. Clarifying questions are helpful here to identify your friend's triggers that lead to their using. You could say, 'what happens to make you want to use?'

Step 3: Reflect Empathetically
Your friend needs your compassion in their time of need. Battling an addiction rarely succeeds without support from others. Show your friend you understand their suffering with, 'your addiction leaves you feeling helpless and alone making it difficult to function,'

Step 4: Offer Validation
Your level of validation in this instance might be to understand their situation from their history of experience. What your friend likely needs from you is either encouragement or support. You could say, 'you've shown

you have the strength to overcome by recognizing the possible future that awaits if you give up the fight.'

Step 5: Confirm Completion
When a friend comes to you for help, you need to give them the opportunity to end the conversation when they are ready. Your goal is to meet their need for reassurance that you are an ally in their fight. Be clear on what you are willing or able to do to help them in their battle with addiction.

Scenario 2
A friend tells you they feel trapped in an abusive relationship. The friend describes the horrible fights filled with screaming and throwing things. You listen as they talk about making a plan to leave.

Step 1: Preparation
A conversation of this magnitude requires your complete attention. Let go of any opinions you have about your friend or their domestic partner. Be ready to commit however much time is needed for your friend to express what they need to say.

Step 2: Listen Attentively
Your friend needs to know you're listening so eye contact and body language are very important. You may find it helpful to ask questions to encourage your friend to keep talking. For example, 'what caused your most recent blow-up?' This can give you insight into the triggers in the relationship that erupt into conflict.

Step 3: Reflect Empathetically
Cognitive empathy is crucial in this type of situation because of the emotional manipulation likely occurring in the relationship. Your friend needs logic and understanding in order to break free from the cycle of

abuse. You could tell your friend, 'you're feeling scared but you're taking steps towards independence and happiness.'

Step 4: Offer Validation

Your level of validation should address the normalness of how your friend is feeling about their situation. The type of validation you choose depends on your level of friendship. For this example, you could express your gratitude for telling you about their situation. You might say, 'I am so glad you've come to me about this because no one should feel afraid at home.'

Step 5: Confirm Completion

Your friend felt safe telling you about their situation. Allow them the time to express any number of emotions they may be feeling right now. Be clear about how you can help them as they continue to prepare for a new life.

Scenario 4

Your friend needs to talk to you about a life changing opportunity. They are excited about changing careers to finally do what they've dreamed of.

Step 1: Preparation

You listen as they tell you about how unhappy their family is about having to move so far away.

Step 2: Listen Attentively

Your friend has conflicting feelings about what to do. You will need to help them sort through and separate their emotions and their source. In this scenario, you will need to include the feelings of your friend's family. This is because how they feel is making your friend feel like they're being torn in two.

Step 3: Reflect Empathetically

What your friend needs is for you to understand their dilema and the two potential outcomes. Your friend may even be feeling guilty for wanting something for themself. You could say, 'you're feeling bad for wanting the new career because of having to uproot your family in order to do what you enjoy.'

Step 4: Offer Validation

You agree that it's normal to feel conflicting emotions when making a major life decision. Anyone would have trouble deciding how to proceed when there are others who will be affected by the decision. Right now, your friend needs a supportive ally. Tell them, 'I'm here for you. Together we can talk to your family and find common ground.

Step 5: Confirm Completion

Your friend has an important decision to make and looked to you for help. Let them decide what more needs to be said or done to resolve their conflict. Make a commitment to talk again, especially if anything changes.

As you can see from these examples, each step plays a critical role in accurately hearing the other person. When you apply the five steps, you are truly committing yourself to the people in your life during their time of need.

Conclusion

You started this journey with a specific goal or two in mind. Maybe you wanted to learn how to be a better listener at work. Perhaps, you hoped to find out why it seems like no one listens to you at home. Or, you want to improve communication with your friends. Whatever your reasons, you took action in a positive direction by reading this book.

I created The Power of Listening in order to open your eyes to the world your ears have been missing. I wanted to show you the depths and complexities of conversation by breaking it down into its basic elements. Each chapter presented concepts to you in a way that made foreign ideas familiar. I gave you a new perspective on what it means to listen and how important it is to feel heard.

You have learned how vital it is for both parties to be prepared for the conversation. The key concept of preparing to listen is mindfulness. Your brain runs at a pretty fast pace. You must learn to channel that energy into staying focused on the conversation taking place. Consciously stopping your mind from drifting off establishes your commitment to the person speaking.

One of the biggest problems we face in today is external distraction. You owe it to the other person to put down your phone or turn off the television and really listen. Healthy communication habits begin with giving your undivided attention. It shows you value the other person and what they want to say when you pause your life to be fully present.

When you prepare for a conversation, you take into account who you're speaking with when choosing your words. Likewise, you factor in how the speaker defines their words in order to better understand the meaning of their message. We each experience life in our own way so you may see excitement where someone else sees terror.

Your mindfulness during the conversation also helps you take notice of the visual cues of their communication. You can read their message so much clearer if you understand the unspoken components of the message. When you are mindful of everything happening in the now, you will find it easier to put all of the pieces together.

As you continued to read the book, you may have found that preparing to listen is by far the easiest of the five steps to effective listening. The second step of active listening requires you to be engaged in the conversation. Your role as an active listener is to fully understand the other person through interaction and respect. Your goal is to get a clear picture of the situation by partaking in the dialogue with intent and purpose.

Here again, body language plays an important role in conveying your attentiveness. You show them you're actively listening with open body posture. You use eye contact and facial expressions to keep focus and express reflective feelings. Your interest and care can also be expressed verbally to learn more about the situation. Or you may seek out details in order to understand their perspective better and find commonality with one another.

You likely discovered several familiar roadblocks that have prevented you from effectively listening in the past. Seeing what has impeded your ability to hear the other person is the first step towards improving interpersonal communication. Being able to understand why these blocks are detrimental makes it easier for you to break those bad habits.

Your empathic abilities are part of what makes up who you are and your humanity. You may be more in tune with cognitive empathy where you relate to how the other person is thinking. Some of you are better at connecting to the emotions of the other person. Or, perhaps you are like those who physically experience the other person's emotional expression with somatic empathy.

However you empathize, you now have a deeper understanding of its role in conversations. You know more about what empathy is and how it enhances relationships. You've also learned that the more you experience in life, the greater you'll be at empathizing with the people in it. You gain a better appreciation for the positives in life when you've witnessed the tragedies of struggle.

Empathy grows out of your ability to see the experience through their eyes. You must be able to perceive the situation from their mindset and think as they do. Being empathic means you refrain from blaming them for their hardships. You acknowledge their experience has any number of factors that influenced the outcome. You're empathic to those you encounter when you respect and cherish the value of humanity.

In our fast-paced instant communication life, we've lost touch with why conversation is important to the health of our relationships. We've forgotten that being connected is strongest when we can relate to one another on a personal level that comes from face to face conversation. We are able to confirm this deeper connection and understanding we have with validation by offering it back.

You share stories of frustration with others, not out of pity, but to confirm the normalcy of your experience. You want to hear from someone else that your experience is exactly as one would expect it to be. Receiving validation that what you feel is real is a justification of your experience. When someone else sees life as you do, then what has happened seems less a personal attack and more of a common occurrence.

Responding to someone's need with validation can be as simple as acknowledging their feelings so they don't feel like they're alone. It may be about showing them you are interested to hear what they're sharing in order to build a stronger relationship. Other times, you'll be needed for words of encouragement or support to help them overcome their fear.

Once you've offered validation to their experience all that remains is bringing the conversation to a clear conclusion. Your power of listening isn't just about hearing the needs of the other person more clearly. It's about taking an active role in your relationships through open and honest communication to address the conflict together.

Your life is intertwined with any number of individuals at home, at work, and in society. You now have the tools of conversation and a greater wealth of knowledge as to how to use them correctly. You're not always going to know exactly what to say, but the more you try the better you'll get. And with any new skill, you need to practice consistently to be your best.

Right now you have a choice to make. You can toss this book on a shelf with an attitude that this will never work. Then you can slip back into your old habits that have caused conflicts and broken relationships. At which point you'll be back to missing the message or not being heard. Or you can take to heart the information you've read and put it to work.

You have an amazing opportunity before you to see humanity in a golden light. Conversations are more than just words exchanged between two people. You have seen how impactful communication can be when fueled by hurt and anger. Be one of the few who have awakened to how powerful conversations can be when nourished with empathy and compassion.

Put down the cell phone. Turn off your computer or television. Change the way you listen to others and soon you'll find the world stopping to listen to you. I wish you all the best!

References

Chapter 1

Lindberg, Sara. "What's the Difference Between Hearing and Listening?" *Healthline*, 27 Sept. 2018, www.healthline.com/health/hearing-vs-listening.

Maranto, Rico. *The Three Levels of Listening*. e-book, PeopleCore Inc., 2020.

Body Language: Beyond Words – How to Read Unspoken Signals." *Mind Tools*, www.mindtools.com/pages/article/Body_Language.htm. Accessed 13 May 2021.

Chapter 2

"Active Listening | SkillsYouNeed." *Skills You Need*, www.skillsyouneed.com/ips/active-listening.html. Accessed 13 May 2021.

Pantazi, Joanna. "The 12 Blocks to Active Listening." *Youniversetherapy*, 29 Sept. 2019, www.youniversetherapy.com/post/the-12-blocks-to-active-listening.

Gray, PhD, Doug. "The Importance of Active Listening – VIEWPOINT Magazine." *Viewpoint Magazine*, 9 July 2019, verdenviewpoint.com/2019/07/the-importance-of-active-listening.

Widrich, Leo. "The Science of Smiling & Why It's So Powerful | Buffer Blog." *Buffer Resources*, 24 June 2020, buffer.com/resources/the-science-of-smiling-a-guide-to-humans-most-powerful-gesture.

Barnard, Dom. "Active Listening Skills, Examples and Exercises." *Virtual Speech*, 20 Sept. 2017, virtualspeech.com/blog/active-listening-skills-examples-and-exercises.

(c) Copyright skillsyouneed.com 2011–2021. "Reflecting - Effective Communication Skills | SkillsYouNeed." *Skills You Need*, www.skillsyouneed.com/ips/reflecting.html. Accessed 13 May 2021.

"Standing Positions And Their Hidden Meaning." *The Only Book On Body Language That Everybody Needs To Read*, bodylanguageproject.com/the-only-book-on-body-language-that-everybody-needs-to-read/standing-positions-and-their-hidden-meaning. Accessed 13 May 2021.

Fritscher, Lisa. "Eye Contact: What You Need To Know | Everyday Health." *EverydayHealth.Com*, 15 Nov. 2017, www.everydayhealth.com/healthy-living/eye-contact-what-you-need-know.

Goman, Carol Kinsey. "The Art and Science of Mirroring." *Forbes*, 25 June 2011, www.forbes.com/sites/carolkinseygoman/2011/05/31/the-art-and-science-of-mirroring.

Chapter 3

"7 Tips for Empathic Listening." *Crisis Prevention Institue*, www.crisisprevention.com/Blog/7-Tips-for-Empathic-Listening. Accessed 13 May 2021.

Schmitz, Terry. "Empathy – Empathetic Listening." *The Conover Company*, 20 Apr. 2021, www.conovercompany.com/empathy-empathetic-listening.

Geekmaster. "Seven Actionable Tips To Boost Your Empathy And Become More Empathetic." *Geeknack*, 18 Jan. 2021, www.geeknack.com/2021/01/17/seven-actionable-tips-to-boost-your-empathy-and-become-more-empathetic.

Cherry, Kendra. "Why Empathy Is Important." *Verywell Mind*, 2 May 2020, www.verywellmind.com/what-is-empathy-2795562.

Indeed Editorial Team. "Empathic Listening: Definition, Examples and Tips." *Indeed Career Guide*, 8 Feb. 2021, www.indeed.com/career-advice/career-development/empathic-listening.

Lamothe, Cindy. "Become an Empathic Listener in 10 Steps." *Healthline*, 17 Nov. 2019, www.healthline.com/health/empathic-listening.

Salem, Richard. "Empathic Listening." *Beyond Intractability*, 28 Feb. 2017, www.beyondintractability.org/essay/empathic_listening.

Chapter 4

Williams, Jennifer A. "How to Talk to Someone with Empathy—and What to Avoid!" *Heartmanity*, blog.heartmanity.com/how-to-talk-to-someone-with-empathy-and-what-to-avoid. Accessed 13 May 2021.

Spitz, Enid R. "The Three Kinds of Empathy: Emotional, Cognitive, Compassionate." *Heartmanity*, blog.heartmanity.com/the-three-kinds-of-empathy-emotional-cognitive-compassionate. Accessed 13 May 2021.

Wilding, Melody. "7 Habits of Highly Empathetic People." *Inc.Com*, 5 Jan. 2021, www.inc.com/melody-wilding/7-habits-of-highly-empathetic-people.html.

Click, Laura. "31 Empathetic Statements for When You Don't Know What to Say." *Medium*, 22 Mar. 2021, blog.usejournal.com/31-empathetic-statements-for-when-you-dont-know-what-to-say-edd50822c96a.

Chapter 5

Vahtra, Tuuli. "A Step by Step Guide to Validating Emotions and Feelings." *Tuuli Vahtra*, 5 May 2020, tuulivahtra.com/a-step-by-step-guide-to-validating-emotions-and-feelings.

Hall, PhD, Karyn. "Understanding Validation: A Way to Communicate Acceptance." *Psychology Today*, 26 Apr. 2012, www.psychologytoday.com/us/blog/pieces-mind/201204/understanding-validation-way-communicate-acceptance.

Salters-Pedneault, PhD, Kristalyn. "What Is Emotional Validation?" *Verywell Mind*, 26 Apr. 2021, www.verywellmind.com/what-is-emotional-validation-425336.

Sorensen, Michael. "Validation: The Most Powerful Relationship Skill You Were Never Taught." *Michael S. Sorensen*, 17 Nov. 2020, michaelssorensen.com/validation-the-most-powerful-relationship-skill-you-were-never-taught.

Earnshaw, Elizabeth. "6 Types Of Boundaries You Deserve To Have (And How To Maintain Them)." *Mindbodygreen*, 21 July 2019, www.mindbodygreen.com/articles/six-types-of-boundaries-and-what-healthy-boundaries-look-like-for-each.

Made in the USA
Las Vegas, NV
02 November 2024

11036183R00075